MURDER IN THE MONTO

Best Wishes
Martin Coffey

Written and compiled by

Martin Coffey B.A. (Hons)

"When you are married

And your husband is cross

Take up the poker

And say I'm the boss"

Private W. Foran

1/7 Gordon Highlanders WWI

Contents

Dedication

This book is dedicated to my grandmother, **Annie Carroll** and to her brother, **Joe Finn** who, because of their mother's involvement in a murder in 1896, spent more time in Industrial Schools than their mother spent in prison for her role in a murder.

It is also dedicated, in the way of an apology, to the memory of **Bridget McKenna** and her children. Her husband, **John** was murdered by a member of my own family in 1896. He was in the wrong place at the wrong time with the wrong people.

Thank you

Gerry Walsh KSG, Dr. Thomas Kador PhD, Terry Fagan and Brendan Coffey, also Gregory O'Connor and Brian Donnelly of the National Archives Ireland, Irishnewspaperarchivesonline, and the staff of Choice Publishing, Drogheda.

Front cover: *Nannie McLoughlin in Grangegorman Prison, 1896,*

© **National Archives, Dublin.**

Back cover: Martin Coffey, Gloucester Street, Jersey.

Prologue

Quite by accident, I came across a report about the murder of a John McKenna that had occurred in Dublin in 1896. As I read through the report, one name in particular jumped off the page, that of Margaret Carroll. I knew from previous research that my great grandmother was a Margaret Carroll and I wondered if this could be one and the same person, as this murder had occurred in Gloucester Lane, close to where my family once lived in city centre Dublin in 1896.

I also knew that Margaret Carroll's daughter, my grandmother, Annie Carroll had spent most of her young life in an Industrial School in County Tipperary but no one in my family seemed to know why she came to be there, not even Annie's daughter, my own mother. Could this murder be the reason why?

One family story told of a fire in a tenement house where Margaret Carroll and her family supposedly lived and that a child had died as a result of the fire. The story goes on to tell of the dead child's mother and father being viewed by the authorities as unfit parents. Two other children belonging to this couple were sent away, placed in an orphanage and Annie Carroll was supposedly one of these two children. But no-one knew for certain if this story was fact or fiction and nobody in my family ever mentioned any connection to a murder. Both of my parents were born in what is now known as Dublin's North Inner City and over the years they told me many stories of their time growing up in this area, surrounded by Tenement Houses, Prostitutes, Brothels and Shebeens. Some of these stories form a part of this book. So, it didn't seem too improbable a leap of faith for me to make in trying to connect this murder to my mother's family. But connected it is and in more ways than one.

One of the ideas that came to my mind when putting all of this research and information into a readable context was to see if it was at all possible to show how three or four generations of Margaret Carroll's family were affected by her role in this murder. I was also curious to know whatever became of all those other people involved. It came as something of a shock to discover that two of the accused had died in prison. The actions of Margaret Carroll and her involvement in this murder still resonate down to the present day, over 120 years later. By way of introduction to this drama, I felt it was necessary to take the reader back in time, to the Dublin of 1896, the year of the murder, in order to get a sense of what life was like for all of those involved, to learn something of what Dublin was like back then and to look at the way in which these people lived and interacted with each other. With great success I researched Newspaper Archives and original Prison Records in search of further information and possible photographs of those imprisoned for their role in this murder.

A major part of the final chapters is about the fall-out from the actions of Margaret Carroll and the way in which it further affected her family. And whatever became of Bridget McKenna, and her six young children, as they too had a price to pay.

Chapter 1

Setting the Scene

A murder in Dublin was not unusual back in the mid to late 1800's but what is unusual in this particular murder case is the fact that two sisters, Margaret Carroll and Nannie McLoughlin were involved in the crime, one of which, Nannie McLoughlin, should possibly have faced the *'Hangman's Noose'* for her role in the taking of an innocent man's life. On Saturday, the 4th July 1896, six people in total were originally arrested and charged with the murder of John McKenna, a charge that was later reduced, for all involved, to manslaughter. During the court hearing, one of the accused, Thomas P. Higgins was proved innocent and released without charge. Margaret Carroll served three years of a five year sentence with penal servitude and her sister, Nannie McLoughlin who was sentenced to seven years penal servitude, was also released early.

Two more of the original accused died in prison, one of which ended up as a patient in Dundrum Mental Asylum where he died insane. And whatever became of Margaret Carroll's three young children, because they too were victims of their mother's actions, two of them served a sentence of more years than their mother, being confined to Reform Schools for a minimum of 8-10 years, with no early release. Her youngest child died while she was away.

To set the scene for this gruesome murder and to help us understand the surrounding social setting of that period, we must step back into a time and place where prostitution was rife, where murder was an almost everyday occurrence and life on the streets of Dublin City was cheap. This particular area of the city was no bigger than an average football field of small dark streets, side lanes and alleyways. The name of each of these streets was well known to Soldiers, Sailors, the Gentry and Hackney Men alike. When King Edward VII of England was Prince of Wales, he was a regular visitor to the Monto. It is also said that two of Ireland's literary giants, James Joyce and Oliver Saint John Gogarty were frequent visitors to this area. British soldiers and merchant seamen from foreign shores made up most of the regular customers who came to this area in search of prostitutes, cheap drink and lustful pleasures in any one of the many Shebeens and Brothels that lined these streets. From 1860 to 1920 there was anything up to 1,600 prostitutes working in this area.

In twenty years from the date of this murder, Dublin would see no less than 16,000 British soldiers on its streets, mainly surrounding the G.P.O. in Sackville Street (O'Connell Street) and other areas, in a fight with Irish Rebels. For the prostitutes of Dublin, this must have seemed like an almost endless supply of ready-made customers.

This was *'The Monto'*, a name derived from Montgomery Street, now present day Foley Street. It was an area of the City of Dublin that at one time was considered the biggest epicentre of prostitution in the then British Empire. It was hemmed in on four sides by Gardiner Street, Summerhill, Buckingham Street and Amiens Street.

James Joyce and Oliver Saint John Gogarty were frequent visitors to the Monto. The Monto was famous long before Joyce ever gave it a mention in his writings.

In some areas there were underground tunnels connecting one side of a street to another, thus providing an easy and quick escape route out of a brothel if a police raid ever occurred. Prospective customers could be seen to walk in through the door of one house and exit the door of a house across the street in the hope that no one would be any the wiser to their business.

The main thoroughfare in this area was most probably present day Railway Street which was once known as Mecklenburg Street/Tyrone Street. Over a period of years, many of these street names changed two or three times. Other well-known streets are Mabbott Street/Corporation Street, now known as James Joyce Street, Little Martin's Lane/Beaver Street, Purdon Street, Elliott

Punters and Prostitutes came in all shapes and sizes.

Monto children.

Place, Faithful Place, Grumlin's Court, White's Lane and Byrne's Square/The Man-Trap. This last lane was situated at the back of Jack Meagher's pub, which was located on the corner of Corporation Street and Purdon Street, it led into Byrne's Square. The prostitutes brought their unsuspecting male clients, sailors, soldiers or otherwise into this lane on the pretence of doing business. She would have organised a few of the local thugs to beat up and rob the poor unsuspecting victim of all he was worth.

On other occasions the client might be asked to remove his trousers and the prostitute would offer to hold onto his coat or jacket for him. While the poor fellow was in the process of unbuttoning himself she would run, with the coat of course and your man's wallet, in through the back door of Jack Meagher's pub and disappear into the crowd inside. Very few men, if any, were brave enough to follow her into the pub and accuse her of stealing his coat, especially while she was sitting amongst her group of like-minded friends sipping a glass of porter. Present day Gloucester Diamond and Sean McDermot Street also played a major role in the history of this area where there are reports of more brothels and shebeens.

The Monto was an area of Dublin that never slept, where neighbours kept a constant and vigilant look out, day and night for strangers or policemen alike. In daylight hours the streets were filled with the noise of young children running about, playing their childish games, mother's leaned out of upstairs windows to keep a

© Martin Coffey

***Stockings and Nylons were a part of the trade of prostitutes in the
Monto in 1896.***

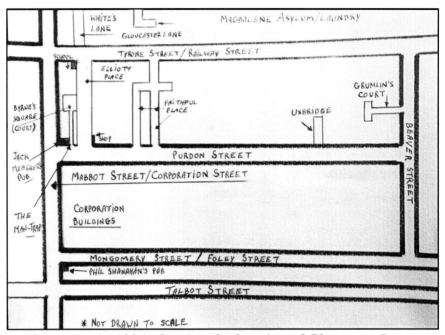

The Monto in 1896, showing the location of Gloucester Lane.

close eye on their children down below and to shout down words of correction to them when they misbehaved. The men of the neighbourhood mainly gathered around a street lamp outside a pub or sat on the step of a doorway leading into a tenement house. They had no money and no work to go to; they were mainly dockworkers who depended on the ebb and flow of the shipping industry for a living. There were however, many hard working families living in this area and good living people too, who were not involved in the seedier side of life. A lot of families and individuals ended up living in this area through no fault of their own and so brothels were now to be found in tenement houses that also contained some of these respectable families.

SHEBEENING.

In the Northern Division of the Police Courts, before Mr Keys, over a dozen shebeen cases were heard. The defendants were men and women residing in tenement houses in Gloucester lane and Mabbot street. In each case numbers of bottles of stout were found concealed on the premises by the prosecuting constables. Fines varying from 20s to 10s were imposed with alternative periods of imprisonment of a fortnight or seven days. In one case the defendant was let off with a caution.

Sergeant 23 C, who prosecuted in this case, said when he entered defendant's place in Gloucester lane he found several bottles of stout there. Some of these had been opened. The defendant, a woman, asked him to have a bottle himself (laughter). He refused the offer. The woman denied that she had the porter for sale; it was All Hallow-Eve, and the liquor had been got in to celebrate the occasion.

Mr Keys said that having regard to the noble offer of the women to give the Sergeant a drink he would dismiss the case with a caution (laughter).

A report from 10th November 1896 relating to tenement houses and Shebeens in both Gloucester Lane and Mabbott Lane.

The Dublin Metropolitan Police in action.

Less than ten years previous to this particular murder, the Whitechapel District of London was in the fearsome grip of '*Jack the Ripper*', the most notorious of Victorian serial killers. The Whitechapel District was very similar to that of Dublin's Monto District, both being increasingly overcrowded and impoverished areas.

In October 1888, London's Metropolitan Police Service estimated that there were 62 brothels and 1,200 women working as prostitutes in Whitechapel. Between the 1860's and the 1920's the Monto was reckoned to house somewhere in the region of 1,600 prostitutes and had an untold number of brothels and Shebeens. Most Dublin prostitutes would have heard stories or read of the horrific deaths of the Whitechapel prostitutes and been very aware of the dangers that they too could possibly find themselves in every time they went out to work the streets. They were living life on the edge, in the extreme.

From the mid 1800's to the early 1900's the vast majority of Dublin people lived in horrendous conditions of dirt, filth and squalor. A later census return shows that 26,000 families lived in inner-city tenement houses and 20,000 of these families lived in just one room. Unlike many people from outside of the Monto, the people that lived here saw no shame in prostitution or shebeens; to them it was just a way of life, a way to survive the hunger pangs of destitution. There was no other way of life for these poor people; they were forever locked inside a poverty trap that showed no mercy.

'Good Time Charlie' hoping to strike a bargain.

© Martin Coffey

A description of a bedroom in the Monto.

"We lived in number 11 Elliott Place. My mother would open the door and there would be the foot of the bed and the other end went up to the window, that's how long the room was. Then just over in the corner was the Chair-Bed, it used to open out for my brother to sleep on. Me and my sister slept at the end of my mother's bed, it was just a single type of bed, my mother slept up at the top with me father and the baby. And then there was the fireplace and a small Kitchen Dresser, and the table was up at the bed, they were all small rooms. There was nowhere to move in it. We'd eat our dinner sitting on the bed. We used to keep the bucket for our toilet out on the Landing. Me father played the Mouth Organ".

Chapter 2

Monto Babies

Young infants and children belonging to unmarried prostitutes were often left inside a tenement doorway in the hope that some kind-hearted neighbour would take them in and rear them as part of their own family. These unwanted children became known as *'Monto Babies'*. These babies were given the new family name and treated the same as if they were born into the family. It sometimes happened that young children were abandoned in these streets by others from outside the area. A mother or father or perhaps a friend or relative, would walk down one of these streets in search of an empty doorway or an empty tenement hallway where they could leave a child and walk away empty-handed.

When it was brought to the attention of the Parish Priest that a child had been *'Taken In'* by a couple, he would make sure that the child was christened but nobody ever ensured that the child's name was registered. Many of these children grew up unaware that the prostitute standing outside the door of their tenement house was in fact their real birth mother.

These poor unfortunate waifs were either cared for by a family from the area or else they would end up in one of the many orphanages situated around Dublin. People often *'took in'* some of these children while their mothers were in prison and the children would all cuddle up together in the same bed each night with children belonging to the original family, most times sleeping on an old sack filled with straw, it was known as a *'Polly Ass'*. Some of these unwanted babies were possibly the result of rape or incest.

Alleged Child Murder in Dublin
27th October 1894

'This afternoon in the Southern Police Court, a young girl named Mary Power was charged with the murder of her female infant child in a house in 3 Erne Terrace. Mrs Mary Rousiter, 12 Burgh Quay stated that she resided in the house, 3 Erne Terrace where she kept a lodging house for servant girls. The prisoner whom she had known for three months came to her house on that evening. Witness then deposed in detail how the accused had been delivered of a child, and her finding it in a closet in the yard. Police Constable 67B gave evidence as to the taking of the dead body of the child out of the closet.

Sergeant 9B deposed to seeing the prisoner on the night in question, when she admitted having given birth to a child. She said that she did not know why she left it in the water to drown. He then took her to the Coombe Hospital. When formally charged with the murder the prisoner said "I did not kill the child."

Doctor Cole-Baker, of the Coombe Hospital, deposed that when he saw the accused she presented the appearance of having been recently delivered of a child, and Doctor Fottrell deposed that death was due to suffocation and not to drowning. He believed that the child had breathed about once or twice after having been born. There were no signs of violence on the body'.

In 1896 the Dublin Coroner reported that in number 16 Ardee Street a baby, who was born alive, was found dead in a closet.

In 1896 a new born child was found dead and floating in the River Liffey.

Every Madam in the Monto had her 'Minder' to protect her from danger and threats.

'And what's your real name…'

On the 31st December 1896 *a child, who was born dead, was found in the Royal Canal near Phibsborough.*

1896: The Coroner reported *that a new baby, found in a doorway, had died from strangulation.*

1896: *Between one and two o'clock in the day, William Hassell, a garden boy at the Chief Secretary's Lodge, was working in the western end of the Demesne, when he found the dead body of a female infant, about four days old, wrapped in a piece of Calico and lying in the shrubbery. The matter was reported to the Police who took charge of the body.*

In 1897 The Coroner reported *that another child died from starvation by its parents.*

In March of 1897 *it was reported that a Servant Girl named Julia Keogh was charged with having attempted to murder her female infant by throwing it into the canal at Herbert Place.*

In May of 1897 *a one year old male child, from number 37 Upper Tyrone Street was found drowned and decomposed in the River Liffey.*

Deserted Child Dead.

Yesterday it was reported to the police by the master of the North Dublin Union, that the deserted child found in the hall of a tenement house in Kendrick street had died. The Coroner has been communicated with.

Infant Found.

Last night Eliza Colgan, 8 Charles street, found a male infant about three days old in the porch of the Franciscan Church, Merchants' quay. It was taken to St Audoen's Church, where it was baptised, and then conveyed to the South Dublin Union.

Dublin Newspaper Report 1898.

On the 8th of October 1898, Anthony Richards and Teresa Hyland were charged on remand for the attempted murder of an infant, Mary Gill, a newly born baby from Gloucester Street, Dublin.

On the 30th of May 1899, a 26 year old mother, Mary Byrne was charged with boiling her newly born child, a baby girl, almost to a pulp in order to more effectively get rid of it. She claimed that the baby was stillborn and that she had given it away to some men.

Drunken Father in 1905

In 1905 Patrick Boshell, with an address in Great Ship Street was charged with causing the death of his infant daughter. His wife told the court that he came home drunk. She and her children became frightened by his drunken behaviour and had to leave the house. Their baby, Agnes was asleep in the bed and sometime later a family member returned to the house and found Boshell fast asleep and lying across the infant. Doctor Ashe stated that the child died from suffocation from the father lying on top of it.

Charge of Infanticide.

The charge against Anne Maher, of 14 George's place, who recently confessed to burying her living infant under a manure heap was, on the application of Mr Clegg (who appeared for the Crown), adjourned till 2 o'clock on Tuesday. Mr Scott defended.

Child killed under Manure Heap.

Three young girls in Elliott Place.

DEAD CHILD FOUND ON DOOR-STEP

Last night a man living at 4 Prebend street found a bundle containing the dead body of an apparently newly-born female child on his doorstep. The body was taken to Richmond Hospital, where it was examined and found to have been dead for some hours.

An inquest was held at the hospital to-day, and a verdict of death from neglect was returned.

Baby died from neglect in 1896.

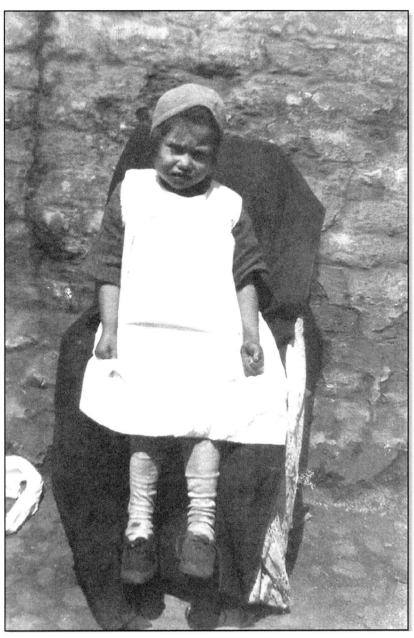

This young girl was once a Monto Baby, she was found behind the hall door of a tenement house in Railway Street, where she had been abandoned.

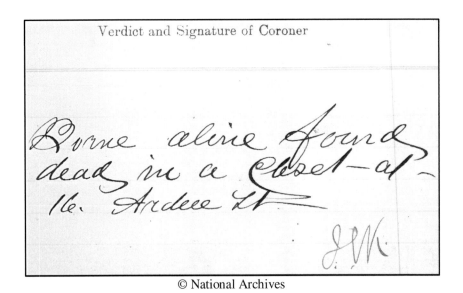

New born child found dead in a closet 1896.

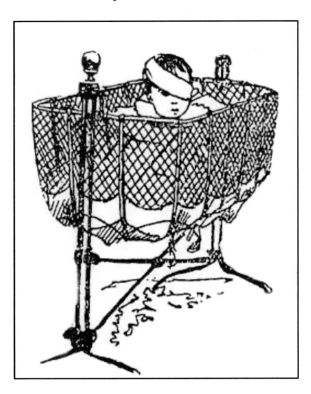

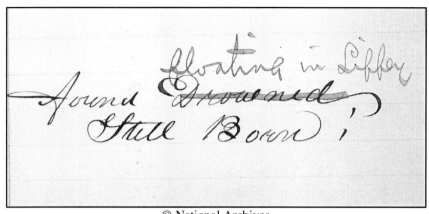

Stillborn baby found floating in the River Liffey 1896.

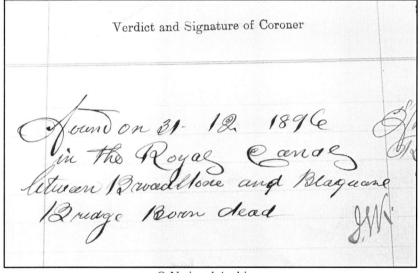

This poor little child was found in the Royal Canal extension that carried water from the main canal in Phibsborough to Broadstone. Today, this area now forms part of the Public Park that leads out to Blessington Street and is known as 'The Basin'. It can be accessed by a series of steps that run alongside the old 'State Cinema' in Phibsborough.

Number 14 Elliott Place was a Shebeen run by Maggie Doyle.

1930's photograph of Monto children, Bessie McKeever, Chrissie Doyle, Mary Anne Doyle, Barney Doyle, Paddy Gorman and Blacker Doyle.

22

Child abuse was often rampant in the Monto.

Chapter 3

Violent Dublin

At the time of the murder of John McKenna in 1896 most people depended on oil lamps and candles to light up their houses and rooms. Each tenement house shared a common water tap, situated down below in the backyard. The toilet facilities were also situated there and were commonly shared by every family in the house. These toilets were rarely emptied by the local authorities cleansing department, thus encouraging large rats to frequent the area, spreading disease and sickness amongst the people.

The vast majority of these giant tenement houses, where up to twenty families or more lived, where uncared for by their owners and some were even in danger of collapsing. Two storey houses lined the smaller, less obvious side streets and lanes where many of the rooms were also inhabited by families with young children. It was also in some of these small houses that many prostitutes carried out their trade.

The Dublin Metropolitan Police Arrest Books for 1905-1918 recorded at least 100 women from one small side street, Elliott Place being arrested and charged with prostitution. This however, is only a portion of the true figure. The 1901 census shows a total of 68 people living in this street, numbers one, eleven and fifteen had six families living in each house. Elliott Place connected Purdon Street with Railway Street. Nearby Faithful Place was in a similar condition to Elliott Place, being filled to overflowing with brothels, prostitutes and shebeens. Railway Street, Purdon Street and Montgomery Street ran parallel to each other and stretched from Corporation Street to Beaver Street. A boundary wall ran along the entire length of Purdon Street. Behind the wall was Corporation Buildings, a type of housing complex, commonly known as *'The Cage'*, due to its likeness in structure to a prison. In the Monto area, families and individuals would often move from one room to another or from one house to another, depending on how low their rent was or how much bigger the room might be. Sometimes, as much as three generations of the one family lived in a single room.

© Martin Coffey

The Monto was an area of Dublin that never slept.

It was not unknown for two families to share one room, with a bed-sheet hung up to divide the space. None of the stairways or landings had any kind of light and there was always a constant smell of unwashed bodies, boiled cabbage and stale Porter hanging in the air over the stairs where prostitutes often sat, while they waited for a customer to come along.

In the early 20th century almost every house in Elliott Place, Purdon Street and in nearby Faithful Place had at least one prostitute living in it. Young children were sometimes used as a ploy by prostitutes. A child would climb up onto the bed and pretend to be asleep and when the customer came in he would be invited to have a drink until the child woke up. After a while he'd get fed up and leave. The prostitute would first make sure that he paid her for her time, be it good or otherwise. If he refused to pay up, there was always her '*Minder*' waiting outside the door with a weapon of some sort or other in his hand, to convince the customer to part with his cash.

When Frank Duff, founder of the Legion of Mary and the City Father's finally closed down the Monto brothels many prostitutes had nowhere to live. One prostitute in particular, known as '*Ginger Kate*', took to sleeping on the bare floor at the top of a stairway in number 11 Elliott Place. One of the married women in the house, Annie Carroll took pity on Kate and offered her a place to live and sleep, under the kitchen table. Kate was glad of the offer and quickly moved in, Annie was the daughter of Margaret Carroll.

© Martin Coffey

The front upstairs room in number 11 Elliott Place was supposedly haunted. The ghostly figure of a man, who was murdered in this room, was sometimes seen standing by the door.

27

Looking up Elliott Place towards Railway Street, house number 10 stood on this corner. The street lamp was a favourite haunt where prostitutes stood, waiting to be picked up.

Underground tunnels discovered in the Monto.

SAVAGE ASSAULT ON A WOMAN.

Three men, named Thomas Clarke, Stephen Byrne, and Joseph Barter, were charged with having savagely assaulted a woman named Mary Anne Roynnane, of Lower Tyrone street, at an early hour on Sunday morning. It was alleged that Clarke struck her on the head, knocking her down, when all three kicked her, and that Barter stabbed and cut her under the chin with a knife. The injured woman had to be conveyed to Jervis street Hospital for treatment. After hearing the evidence Byrne was discharged, and Clarke and Barter were each sent to jail for two months with hard labour.

A savage assault in 1895.

'Get home to your wife and leave my daughter alone…'

And that's the way it was for many more prostitutes and homeless people from the Monto. A Dublin Metropolitan Police Report from 1892 stated that in 1889, 1,355 women were arrested for prostitution, in 1890 the figure was 1,077 and in 1892 this figure was at its lowest with only 948 prostitutes being arrested. In 1893 eight males were charged with murder but only one was convicted and sentenced to death. Twenty two males and three females were arrested for manslaughter, 325 people were arrested for striking a Policeman. There were 479 known thieves at large in the city.

In October of 1896, Anne Wade was up before the magistrate on a charge of neglecting and deserting her two children, Eliza age 8 years and Mary age 5 years, by The Society for the Prevention of Cruelty to Children. Both of the children were eventually placed in the care of the Dublin Union. The court was told that this was one of the worse cases that the Society had ever come across. The prisoner and her husband were to attend before the Magistrate to answer the charge. The children's mother it was stated was training her eldest daughter to be a prostitute. Their young son was forced to beg in the street while pretending to be blind.

On Thursday, the 9th March 1893, Christopher Smith was charged with murder by strangulation of his wife in their home in Tara Street, Dublin.

On Saturday the 15th April 1893, 26-year-old Ellen Bolger was charged with the murder of her infant child by throwing the baby into the canal.

On Monday, the 10th July 1893, Edward Leigh was executed in Kilmainham jail for the murder of an old woman, Bridget Knight of Kimmage.

On Wednesday, the 2nd August 1893, James Reilly from Stepaside was charged with the wilful murder of an old man, Bernard Cox

On Wednesday, the 17th October 1894, Michael Dowling was charged with the wilful murder of Denis Kinsella, an inmate of the Richmond Lunatic Asylum.

On the 26th of January 1895, John Doran was charged on remand with having wilfully killed his twelve month old stepson, Christopher Kavanagh, by seizing the infant by the neck. One witness said he heard the child's mother screaming "My child, my child."

Robbery with violence 1896: John Lyons, a Private in the 13th Hussars and Kate Smith of 14 Montgomery Street, were charged, in custody of Constable 139C, with robbing with violence in the house mentioned from a sailor named Stolie, of 5 shillings and some clothing. Stolie deposed that Lyons struck him down and that he was then stripped and robbed. The prisoners were returned for trial.

On the 11th of April 1896, Patrick Brennan pleaded not guilty to the killing and slaying of Thomas Morrissey at a house in Ash Street, Dublin

The very threat of being sent to an Industrial School was sometimes enough to make young boys behave themselves.

'**A ten year old** boy named Michael O'Brien of Brady's Cottages off Mabbott Street, was charged by Constable 32C with the theft of a Pawn Ticket for a silver Geneva watch from Thomas Bassett, who was drunk under the archway. The Constable alleged that he saw the boy searching Bassett's pockets while the latter lay drunk. When arrested the Pawn Ticket was in the boys possession. The parents of the boy, with tears in their eyes, appealed for mercy on the boy. The father said that this was the boys first offence and blamed it on bad example.

Mr. Carton said the father seemed respectable and was standing in the boy's light in opposing him being sent to an Industrial School. The Policeman said that the boy's occupation was going on messages for unfortunate women. The boy's father denied all knowledge of this.

Mr. Carton said this ought not to be unknown to the parents. He would send the boy to Artane or Carriglea Industrial Schools. More serious than the offence by which the lad was charged was the fact that he was keeping company with infamous women'

'**Thirty years old** John Woods was charged with assault on his wife and infant. He punched his wife about the head and body and then threw the six month old infant across the bed, striking its head off the wall. The child had to be taken to hospital. His wife said that her husband had drunk a pint of whiskey before the assault. He was sentenced to six months with hard Labour'.

On the 18th May, 1896, a Fish Dealer named Mary Lacken was remanded on a charge of murdering her 16-year-old son, John. Her son complained at breakfast that his eggs were not properly cooked. Mrs Lacken was busy cleaning out fish at the time and threw a large scissors at him. This struck her son in the shoulder and caused a massive wound from which he died a few minutes later.

'She cleaned me out Officer...'

On Wednesday, the 2nd December 1896, 64-year-old Thomas Heenan was charged with the wilful murder of his wife at their home in 16 Kenilworth Square, Dublin.

December 1897: Mary Anne Goodman was charged with abandoning her infant child by leaving it in number 11 Elliott

Place. Police Sergeant Donohoe received information and went to the address where he found the child. He then traced the mother and arrested her.

February 1892: Anne Green of Montgomery Street was charged with stealing 90 pounds from a farmer who said he was on his way to America. She was also charged with illegally possessing five gold watches, two chains, a locket and a Revolver.

August 1899: William Ryan from Montgomery Street was charged with the illegal possession of three and a half stone of Gutted Lead. He was remanded for a week.

May 1895: Anne Wolfe and Mary Anne Malone were charged with stealing £210 from Patrick Morgan in a brothel in Montgomery Street. Morgan was a Grocer and Provision dealer from the country and was in Dublin on business.

August 1907: Catherine Brown was accused of murdering her child by drowning in a crock of water. One witness said that she saw Mrs Brown sitting in the room on an old axle with the baby on her lap and the child's head in the crock of water. A Police Sergeant said that she was of unsound mind when he came upon the scene. The jury found her guilty of manslaughter and asked the court to show her mercy. She was given a six month prison sentence.

A Dublin Jarvey waiting on his passenger in the Monto.

On the 1ˢᵗ August 1900, Eliza Goulding was charged with stealing a purse containing 22s 6d and a gold watch from Peter Lanzardi at a house in Elliott Place. The judge remarked that the house seemed to be a 'Den of Thieves' and the prisoner had previously been convicted on 15 times for various offences.

This then, is the world that Margaret Carroll and her sister, Nannie McLoughlin lived in, one that almost ran parallel to that of a Charles Dickens novel where prostitution, thieving and the use and abuse of young children was rampant and where name changing was an everyday occurrence. This was a neighbourhood boiling over with excessive violence, where murder lingered in the air and life came cheap. Dublin, in the 1890's saw more than its fair share of murder and mayhem. The Monto in particular, had become a very dangerous place to be, where no-one was safe and especially if you were a stranger passing through.

How did two country girls, like the Finn sisters manage to end up working in the Monto and how did one of them become a Madam? This was not as unusual as it may first appear. In those years, if a prostitute managed to come into more money than usual they would rent out two or more rooms and sublet to other prostitutes, in this way they then eventually became a Madam.

The vast majority of prostitutes in the Monto came from outside of Dublin, '*Country Girls*', with many coming from institutions such as the Magdalene Laundry situated in nearby Sean McDermot Street. The back entrance to this laundry was situated on Railway

Street. Other prostitutes came from as far away as Liverpool, Glasgow and Manchester.

Madams and their girls worked very closely together, it was dangerous for a girl to step out of line. If they ever did, they could end up being disfigured with the blade of a knife or a broken bottle. When the girls lost their looks they were very often thrown out onto the street to fend for themselves.

It was not unusual for some of the prostitutes to help out families or individuals in the area who were worse off than themselves by giving them whatever spare money they might have. It is also said that if a family were being evicted from their flat for not paying their rent, some of the prostitutes would band together and pay it for them. In this way prostitutes, regardless of where they came from were very much accepted into the community.

When wheeling or dealing with anyone in the Monto it was always wise to try and keep one step ahead of the law.

Foley Street with shawled women and a young child looking in a shop window.

(Courtesy of I.A.C. Ltd)

The skeleton of a 'Monto Horse'.

In 2012 the Cultural Learning Initiative launched an investigation of Dublin's urban landscape of 100 years ago from an archaeological perspective. The first phase of the project focused on daily life in Dublin's north inner city with particular reference to the capital's infamous tenements.

During the excavation of one particular tenement site, situated at the back of James Joyce Street/Corporation Street, they uncovered the skeleton of an old workhorse that evidently had been butchered for meat. The meat was then stripped off its bones and the skeleton buried in the back garden of the tenement house. The poor horse probably died from old age and being overworked.

© Martin Coffey

The name "Monto" is forever associated with Prostitution and Shebeens, a place where murder, violence and abuse lived side by side. This was certainly the case with Nannie McLoughlin and her gang of like-minded thugs when they beat up John McKenna in 1896.

Chapter 4

Murder in the Monto

On Monday, the 6th of July 1896, 24-year-old Margaret Carroll and her 30-year-old sister, Nannie McLoughlin were arrested and charged, along with four other persons, John McLoughlin, husband of Nannie McLoughlin, John Byrne, Annie Higgins and her son, Thomas P. Higgins, for the murder of 43-year-old, John McKenna. The murder took place in the early hours of Saturday morning, the 4th July, in number 3 Gloucester Lane, situated in Dublin's infamous 'Red Light District'.

These were tough people, used to dealing with all sorts of customers and in all sorts of ways. Monto Madam, Nannie McLoughlin had several young prostitutes working for her, each of whom lived in constant fear of her foul and hot temper. She was the boss of the gang that ran this brothel, she laid down the law and made and changed the rules as she saw fit. Nobody crossed or questioned Nannie, not even her husband, if they wanted to live or keep their good looks.

This gang spun a daily web of deceit and lies, trapping anyone and everyone that they could find and enticing them into their den of iniquity. Once they succeeded in gaining the confidence and false friendship of some poor unsuspecting victim, the trap was sprung. These were creatures of the night that never slept as long as there was the possibility of luring an innocent victim into their lair. Under

***Number 3 Henrietta Street, where John McKenna lived with his
wife and young family at the time of his murder in 1896.***

the cover of darkness they operated at their best and were forever
honing their skills. One such victim of these times was 43 year old
John McKenna, a married father of seven young children, who lived
with his wife at number 3 Henrietta Street, Dublin and was
employed as a Boiler Maker with the Midland Great Western

Railway Company, based in nearby Broadstone. McKenna is described as having a big strong frame with powerful muscles and is said to have weighed about 16 stone, a man no doubt, quite capable of taking care of himself in most given situations. He was a '*Hands On*' engineer, used to lifting and shifting heavy steam-engine boilers and not afraid of hard work.

Hard Times and Hard Women.

© Martin Coffey

Inside the hallway of a tenement house in Henrietta Street. Homeless men often slept on the floor in the hallways of the old tenement houses.

What is known about John McKenna is that on one previous occasion he had spent some time in the company of a young 19 year old prostitute from the Monto. It is not known if he had ever spent time with other prostitutes on any previous occasion. This particular evening was to be the beginning of the end for John McKenna when he made a conscious decision to return to the murky underworld of the Monto and play a very dangerous game of cat and mouse with a young prostitute who was well schooled in the art of deception. Like so many men before him, John McKenna would pay a heavy price for the pleasure of a young woman's company. This fly was about to step into the parlour of a very dangerous and lethal Spider.

© Martin Coffey

Jack Meagher's pub, in the heart of Dublin's Monto district. The entrance to 'The Man-Trap' is situated between the back of the pub and the white building seen on the right of this photograph.

On Friday night, the 3rd July 1896, unknown to his wife and family, John McKenna once again sought out the company of this young woman. The prostitute, Carrie Thompson would later tell the court that she rented a room for her business in number 3 Gloucester Lane, from Nannie McLoughlin, one of the accused. It was also here that she lived.

A DUBLIN TRAGEDY

Dublin, Wednesday.

The circumstances surrounding a murder of a very violent character, which took place on the 4th July last, were investigated to-day before Mr Justice Gibson at the City Commission, when John Byrne, John McLaughlin, Margaret Carroll, and Annie Higgins were charged with the murder of John McKenna. From the evidence it appeared that McKenna, Thomas Higgins, and Maurice McLaughlin, who was a married man of about 45 years of age and in the employment of the Midland Great Western Railway, went on the date mentioned to a house of ill-fame in Gloucester lane with a girl named Carrie Thompson. Whiskey was brought in and drunk, and in consequence of some of the prisoners demanding part of the drink a quarrel ensued, during which Carrie Thompson was struck and forced to leave the house. McKenna, who attempted to save her, was fiercely attacked, beaten with a poker, and an instrument which was partly a hammer and partly a hatchet, robbed of all he possessed, and left in an unconscious condition in a dark corner of the lane.

Thomas Higgins was acquitted. The jury found all the other prisoners guilty of manslaughter, and John M'Laughlin and John Byrne were sentenced to ten years' penal servitude, and Anne M'Laughlin and Margaret Carroll to seven years, and Anne Higgins to five years.

Irish Examiner 1896.

She further stated that she was approached by the deceased in nearby Gloucester Street (Sean McDermot Street) on the date in question. She also told the court that she had met the deceased on one previous occasion, close to the same spot where they met on that Friday night. Thompson said that she enjoyed being in McKenna's company. She obviously appealed to McKenna and she may therefore have played on this to entice him further into her trap. Once he was smitten she could then easily lead him along by the nose with the sure knowledge that she could make quite a lot of money out of him. According to Carrie Thompson, John McKenna stood talking to her in Gloucester Street for quite a while before suggesting that they take a walk together out by the seafront at Clontarf, a walking distance of about 1-2 miles. She also stated that, in her estimation John McKenna was not drunk when they met.

Was this visit to Carrie Thompson perhaps a last minute decision by John McKenna or had he planned it sometime before? He obviously enjoyed being in the company of this much younger woman and he was after all, more than twice her age and she was only two years older than his eldest son. Little or nothing is known about his own domestic situation or his relationship with his wife. He was obviously living a lie in regards to his faithfulness to her.

According to a statement later given at the Coroner's Court by Patrick McKenna, son of the deceased, John McKenna had finished work at about five o'clock on Friday evening, the 3rd July 1896. As usual, he arrived home with his weekly wage packet and gave this

Three generations of Monto men.

**White's Lane, off Railway Street, close to where John McKenna
was murdered in 1896.**

© Martin Coffey

***Two 'Monto Babies' sitting on the front step of a tenement house
with their pet hen.***

to his wife, Bridget. Sometime later that evening, at about 7.30pm
John McKenna told his wife that he was going to Redmond's shop
in Gardiner Street to buy a coat. Patrick said that his father had
about 20 shillings with him when he last left home (*There were 20
shillings in a Pound, almost a week's wages to most people in
1896).* and that nothing seemed out of place or unusual on that
evening when he last saw his father alive, they were a normal
everyday family with the usual worries and cares of their time.

So, what was the deciding factor in John McKenna's mind that
brought him to a point where he would seek out, not just once but
twice, a young prostitute for company? And why was he carrying
so much money, had he really intended to buy a new coat, as he led

his wife to believe? Carrie Thompson never told the court what conversations took place between her and John McKenna as they walked along by the seafront or why they didn't just '*get down to business*' when they first met. Perhaps if they had, then this murder may never have taken place.

'Peeping Tom' in the Monto.

Carrie Thompson told the court that after the attack on John McKenna she had spent the rest of that night in Purdon Street and that on her way there she met a Policeman whom she asked to arrest Nannie McLoughlin for assaulting her. She had also spent some time in Jervis Street Hospital having her head wound dressed and it was here that she first mentioned the assault on John McKenna to the hospital staff.

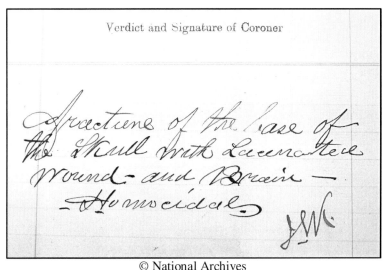

© National Archives

A part of the Coroner's report into the death of John McKenna.

Doctor Lyons, the House Surgeon of the South Dublin Union Hospital stated that the deceased was admitted to the hospital on Saturday morning. He was in a coma from which he never recovered. He further stated that when the deceased was admitted he had a cut on the back of his head and there was bleeding from behind the left ear and from the nose. On further examination of the body he found a fracture at the base of the skull extending from the

"Never mind what your father said..."

left side. There was also a large clot of blood on the brain; the pressure of this clot was possibly the cause of the coma. Doctor Lyons said that very great violence must have been used to cause such damage to the skull. When he was shown the Hammer/Hatchet implement that the Police found on the premises where the murder had taken place, Doctor Lyons said that this instrument would have left a much deeper wound than the one that he found on the skull of the deceased. Having examined this instrument with a magnifying glass, he said that he found no evidence of blood on it. Death, he

Purdon Street, celebrating the 100th anniversary of Catholic Emancipation in 1923.

The two boys are standing outside number 50 Purdon Street; the house behind them is number 51. The taller building just beyond the two carts is a shop, number 9 Elliott Place. Behind the wall on the left is Corporation Buildings.

said was caused by a blow to the base of the skull and that the cut was only an inch deep.

So, if the instrument examined by Doctor Lyons was not the weapon that killed McKenna then it might stand to reason to suggest that the poker used by Nannie McLoughlin was the murder weapon, because according to eyewitness, Carrie Thompson these are the only two weapons used in the carrying out of this crime and she testified that Nannie McLoughlin had struck McKenna with a poker- like instrument. McLoughlin had earlier threatened John McKenna with violence and was overheard to say in a screaming voice that, '*She would do for him*', perhaps meaning that she would not stop until he was dead.

The Coroner said that Gloucester Lane was a cul-de-sac and at about forty yards from the entrance to Gloucester Street it turned at right angles to the left, there were no houses in that part running close to Gloucester Street, with a dead wall at each side. It was mid-way down this part of the lane where John McKenna was found, about thirty yards away from number 3 Gloucester Lane where all of the accused lived. This house was at the back of 95 Tyrone Street by which it was separated by a yard, this was another well-known brothel. This lane is today situated across the road from Our Lady of Lourdes Church in Sean McDermot Street and leads directly into Railway Street. Originally, it only extended halfway along the length of the present day lane, with walls on both sides and turned into the left.

John McLoughlin and Kilmainham Jail 1896.

This is Gloucester Lane in 2016, where John McKenna was found unconscious in 1896. The original lane turned into the left halfway along this pathway and it was here that the murder took place (See following photograph). A wall once stood where the present day railings are on the right. There were no houses in this part of the lane.

The jury found that death was caused by injuries stated in the medical evidence and that the injuries were inflicted by all those in custody, except Thomas Higgins. All of the accused were found guilty of manslaughter. Two of the jury did not sign this verdict, being in favour of an open case, the remaining fourteen did. Margaret Carroll, who stole from McKenna's pockets and Annie Higgins, who held an Oil Lamp for her, were each sentenced to five years with Penal Servitude. Nannie McLoughlin was sentenced to seven years Penal Servitude, her husband; John McLoughlin and John Byrne were each sentenced to ten years Penal Servitude. And so we come to the end of the courtroom drama relating to the untimely death of John McKenna.

*This is the extension of Gloucester Lane where the house once
stood belonging to Nannie McLoughlin, the Monto Madam.
In real terms, the back of her house would face the camera.*

*The entrance to the Brothel at 95 Tyrone Street/Railway Street, at
the rere of Nannie McLoughlin's house, once stood where this
gateway is situated. Gloucester Lane is to the left of this
photograph.*

DUBLIN TRAGEDY.

A MAN WITH A BROKEN SKULL.

Six Arrests.

Late on Friday night Constables 121 C and 62 C, while on beat duty, discovered in Gloucester lane a man lying unconscious in a pool of blood. They immediately took him to Jervis street Hospital on a stretcher, where Dr Lyons, the house surgeon, found he was suffering from fracture of the skull. The man remained unconscious, and died at six o'clock on Saturday morning. The condition of his garments showed that he had been savagely attacked and robbed. His coat was nearly torn off his back; all his pockets had been turned out, and his watch and chain, which had left marks on the clothes, were missing. The police, after much inquiry, finally got the dead man identified. He was a married man named James M'Kenna, aged 43 years. He resided in Henrietta place, and was employed as a boilermaker at the Broadstone Railway Terminus. M'Kenna leaves a wife and seven children. On Saturday morning Sergeants Jas Carroll and Whelan, of the Summerhill station, investigated the affair, and as a result they arrested and preferred the capital charge against John Byrne, John M'Loughlin, John P Higgins, Anne M'Loughlin, Margaret Carroll, alias M'Loughlin, and Anne Higgins. All these people live in 3 Gloucester lane, outside of which the man was discovered. It is stated that shebeen business was carried on in the house. The arrests were due to information unwittingly given by a woman named Carrie Thompson, whilst she was being attended for a wound in the head at Jervis street Hospital.

Newspaper Report on Dublin Tragedy 1896.

Chapter 5

The Madam

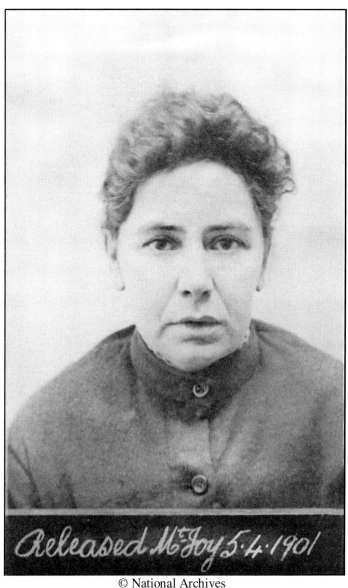

© National Archives

Monto Madam, Nannie McLoughlin in 1901, wearing her prison clothes.

© National Archives

***Prison entry for Nannie McLoughlin, Margaret Carroll and
Nannie Higgins in 1896.***

© Martin Coffey

A Dublin Tenement Doorway.

One of the accused in this murder case is Nannie McLoughlin nee Finn (1862-1932), who like her sister, Margaret was also born in Cloneygowan, Portarlington. At 5 feet 3 inches in height Nannie was the taller of these two sisters. According to the Coroner's Report into this murder, John McKenna died as a result of a blow to the back of his skull; this was the blow with a poker delivered by Nannie McLoughlin. All of the evidence presented to the court, especially from witnesses, points to her deliberately and wilfully setting out to kill John McKenna and yet, she was found guilty of manslaughter. In 1886 Nannie Finn emigrated to America and lived in New York State where she worked as a Domestic Servant. In 1889 she returned to Dublin and later married John McLoughlin in the Pro Cathedral on the 10th March 1890. Witnesses at the wedding

The Monto was full of 'Street Urchins'.

were Joseph Kinahan and Kate McLoughlin. On the marriage certificate for this couple, Nannie states that her father, Leonard Finn was deceased but he was in fact, still very much alive, he didn't die until 1916.

In late 1889 Nannie McLoughlin was arrested for prostitution under the name of Anne McLoughlin, alias Anne Finn, alias Annie Finn, alias, Nannie McLoughlin, alias Annie O'Loughlin, alias Annie Mask, alias Anne Nowland. On the 24th January 1885, 23 year old Anne Finn was up before the bench on a charge of assault. Over the next few years she is charged, on no less than thirteen occasions with theft, assault, drunkenness and abusive language. She spent anything from 14 days to 1 month in prison for most of these offences.

On Monday, the 6th of July 1896, the Dublin newspapers reported that the courthouse in Green Street was packed to overcrowding, with throngs of people outside, gathered on the pavement. Inside, six people, John McLoughlin, his wife Nannie McLoughlin, her sister Margaret Carroll, John Byrne, 42 years old Annie Higgins, a Nurse from Monkstown, County Dublin and her son, Thomas P. Higgins were to stand trial for committing a very violent and gruesome crime, that of the wilful murder of John McKenna. The Chief Crown Solicitors' Department said that the evidence would show a sad story of brutality and violence and made all the sadder by the fact that the deceased was a married man with a young family.

Mister Justice Gibson presided. Also present were the following; Sergeant Dodd and Mister Wright QC (Instructed by Sir Patrick Coll, Chief Crown Solicitor) for the prosecution. Mister Philip Keogh (Instructed by Mister McCune) defended Thomas Higgins. Mister Eustace Johnston (Instructed by Mister Walsh) defended all the other prisoners. Sergeant Dodd opened the case by telling the court that in the early hours of Saturday morning, the 4th July 1896, at about twenty minutes past one o'clock, Sergeant James Freely, while going on his rounds near Gloucester Street, found a man lying on his back on the pavement. Another Police report however, states that John McKenna was found lying face down in the street and unconscious, with his coat beside him and the pockets of it turned

Even the Police were wary of strangers in the Monto.

inside out, as also were his trouser pockets. Sergeant Freely said that he called for assistance and had the man removed to hospital. In a later statement, by Constable Joseph Ward, number 121C, it was stated that a message had arrived at Summerhill Police Station directing him and another Constable to take a stretcher and go to Gloucester Lane to remove a man who was believed to be drunk. He further stated that when they arrived at the scene the individual involved was speechless and snoring. They placed him on the stretcher and took him back to the Police Station.

It was at this point that the two Policemen realised that John McKenna was badly wounded and so they brought him to hospital where he died within a short while of his arrival. Sergeant Freely said that at about four o'clock that morning he went back to the area where John McKenna was found and saw no signs of a scuffle. He said that he came to the conclusion that this was not the scene of a fight and that perhaps John McKenna had been beaten elsewhere and left at this spot by his assailants. He said that he then noticed John McLoughlin and his wife, Nannie at their bedroom window, in number 3 Gloucester Lane. He was suspicious of the fact that the two of them were fully dressed at that hour of the morning.

The sergeant said that he later spoke to one of the Constables back at the Station who had brought John McKenna to hospital and as a result of this conversation he then went back again to where he had seen the McLoughlin's, at about five o'clock on that morning. Sergeant Freely stated that he questioned the two of them about the row in the lane and said that they denied hearing or seeing anything

© Martin Coffey

'I pray the Lord my soul to keep'. Small shrines, similar to the above, were a regular feature of many tenement rooms. Most of the Monto people and their families had great faith in their religion.

of what he asked. Nannie McLoughlin told him that she had spent the night with her mother over in Green Street and hadn't arrived home until about three o'clock that morning. It was at this point in the proceedings that Freely was cross examined by Mister Johnston, who said that Gloucester Street was to the rere of Lower Tyrone Street and that it was not unusual for people in that locality to be up all night. Sergeant Freely then said that when he first came across

McKenna he thought he must have been thrown out of a brothel and had fallen asleep on the ground.

Carrie Thompson had told the court that on their way back from Clontarf, both she and John McKenna went into a pub where McKenna bought a small bottle of whiskey. She said that they drank some of the whiskey as they walked and talked their way back to town. She also stated that it was almost midnight when she and John McKenna arrived at the house where Thompson said she had a room they could use. This was an upstairs room in number 3 Gloucester Lane, a two storey cottage and a well-known brothel and Shebeen run by Nannie McLoughlin and her husband. She also told the court that this was where all of the accused lived.

The judge said that this was not a place where any self-respecting man ought to be found. What, he wondered, was a married man like John McKenna doing out at that hour of the night with a young woman, when he had a wife and family to go home to. Thompson told the court that she brought John McKenna to her upstairs room where they were planning to finish off the night together.

Margaret Carroll then walked into the room where Thompson and McKenna were, in order to disturb any act of intimacy that might be taking place. This was a ploy sometimes used by prostitutes to try and distract a client and get him to leave earlier than he had planned to but have him pay before leaving. The second prostitute would stand in the room talking to the first prostitute, who would either sit on the bed or stand up and pretend to listen to her friend.

After a while the client would usually get fed up waiting and leave, but he was expected to pay the prostitute for her time. In this way, the first prostitute got her money and her client went off empty handed. It was similar to the ploy mentioned earlier about prostitutes using children to put a client off. This was a well-worked routine in this brothel.

It was then that Margaret Carroll noticed the small whiskey bottle sitting on a table beside the bed. Without hesitation she lifted the bottle to her lips and emptied it. This is now the point in the story where everything changes colour, when the dynamics between John McKenna and Carrie Thompson spirals out of control and their worst nightmares begin.

According to Thompson's later testimony, Nannie McLoughlin, the brothel Madam, then came into the room making demands on the young prostitute. McLoughlin also had it in mind to put the squeeze on John McKenna for extra cash, another ploy often used by the Madams who would normally make sure to have at least two of her *'Strong Men'* at her side in order to make the client feel threatened and who would then feel it necessary to meet the demands of the Madam to ensure a safe and quick exit from the brothel. What did John McKenna make of all this, it was after midnight and he had already spent at least five hours in the company of Carrie Thompson. Did he have any thoughts at this stage of going home to his wife and family? And of course all that he had for his money at this stage of the game was a stroll and a chat with the young prostitute and nothing more by all accounts.

'You owe me more than that'.

Visitors to the brothels were often pressurised into paying much more money than they had bargained for.

Neighbours from the Monto.

According to the Police Report, Nannie McLoughlin had come into the room looking for rent money from Carrie Thompson. Having got her money she then noticed the whiskey bottle on the table and demanded a drink. Young Thompson stood and told McLoughlin that the bottle was empty and that there was no whiskey left.

The court was told that Nannie McLoughlin then flew into a mad rage and attacked Carrie Thompson, taking up the whiskey bottle and striking Thompson across the head with it, Carrie Thompson was knocked unconscious with the force of the blow. According to Thompson's testimony, John McKenna tried to shield her from any further blows of the bottle and he told Nannie McLoughlin to leave her alone. She stated that she then fell to the floor where she remained unconscious for some time. When she eventually came around everyone was gone out of the room.

The Madams of the Monto were ruthless in their dealings with young prostitutes. If any of them dare cross them in any way they could end up with broken bones, slashed faces or cigarette burns on their arms or face. Each scar and disfigurement was to act as a warning signal to other prostitutes not to cross the line with their

Derelict tenement houses in Dublin.

Madam. The prostitutes also had to be wary of the Madam's strong arm enforcers. These were the thugs who did as they were ordered, they were the men who provided protection for the Madams and in return were paid for their services to her. Most of these young prostitutes depended on their looks to attract a customer and if they were in any way disfigured then they might not get any business.

Most disputes in the Monto were sorted 'out of court'.

One of these thugs was one-eyed, John McLoughlin, husband of Monto Madam, Nannie McLoughlin; he was her *'Personal Enforcer'* and her Minder. He was generally the rough and tough side of this duo, except in this case when his wife changed the rules of the game and enforced her own style of justice on the heads of Carrie Thompson and John McKenna. When a prostitute was arrested the Police made a note on the Arrest Sheet of any marks, scars or tattoos on the individual involved. On many occasion it is noted there are cut marks on the wrist or lower arm of the prostitute. These may have been caused by self-harm or perhaps they were a warning from the Madam not to step out of line.

The 'Monto Madam' was a law unto herself.

Chapter 6

Margaret Carroll

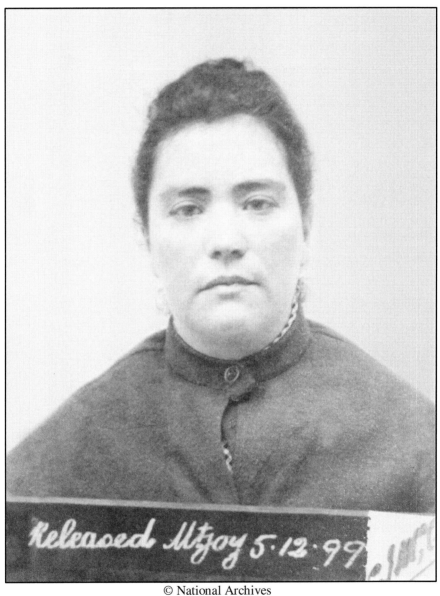

© National Archives

Prison photograph of Margaret Carroll in 1899.

© Martin Coffey

The main gate into Grangegorman Female Penitentiary.

Another of the accused, Margaret Carroll was born on the 5th June, 1870 in Cloneygowan, Portarlington, to Leonard Finn, a shoemaker and his wife, Bridget Foster. Margaret was one of 11 children. At some point in time, when she was a young girl, her parents moved to Dublin. With so many thousands of British Soldiers stationed in Dublin at that time, her father had hoped to put himself in a better position, with his craft of shoemaking and shoe repairing skills, for getting plenty of work. They first lived in a tenement room in number 7 Corn Exchange Place, off Burgh Quay, Dublin. In 1883, 13 year old Margaret Finn was arrested and detained in Grangegorman Women's Prison for stealing a silk handkerchief in North Earl Street. She was less than 5 feet tall with fair hair and grey eyes.

© National Archives

*Grangegorman Penal Record of Prisoner B260, Margaret Carroll,
aka Margaret McLoughlin.*

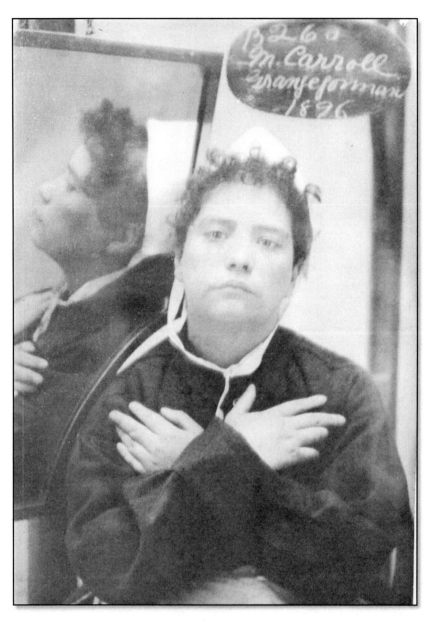

© National Archives

Prisoner B260, 24 year old, Margaret Carroll nee Finn, at the time of her imprisonment in Grangegorman Female Penitentiary in 1896. Her arms are folded across her chest to show that she has all of her fingers. A mirror was used to show her profile.

By 1832 the cholera epidemic was at its height in Dublin and Grangegorman Prison, originally known as the Richmond Penitentiary, was used as a temporary hospital. The Richmond Penitentiary was reopened in April 1837 and was to receive only female prisoners. It was at that time the only prison in Ireland used exclusively for this purpose. It had 256 cells and these were 12 feet square and 11feet in height and would have had several inmates sharing a cell at any one time, adults and children alike. It later became known as the Grangegorman Female Penitentiary.

It was here that a young 13 year old Margaret Finn was held until arrangements were made for her transfer to Spark's Lake Reformatory School for Girls, in County Monaghan. Two weeks after her arrival at Grangegorman Prison, Margaret was moved to Monaghan where she was expected to spend the next five years of her young life. Nothing further is known of Margaret's time spent in Monaghan.

In 1887, Margaret Finn's parents were living in a tenement room in Barrack Street, Dublin (*Present day Benburb Street*). This was situated close to the Royal Army Barracks (*Michael Collin's Museum*) where Margaret's father, Leonard Finn, was working at repairing and making shoes for the army. It was also around this time that 17 year old Margaret Finn gave birth to her first child, Henry Joseph Finn, in the North Dublin Union Workhouse. No father is mentioned on the birth certificate for this child and it may be assumed that the child's father is very possibly a British Soldier or did she perhaps, come back to Dublin from Monaghan pregnant?

Grangegorman Prison cells closely packed together in narrow and dreary walkways.

In 1887 Barrack Street, like the Monto, was another well-known Red Light District of Dublin and being so close to the army barracks was guaranteed a steady supply of young homesick soldiers with money in their pockets, who were probably looking for plenty of drink and lots of female company. In Barrack Street there was an endless supply of both.

Sparks Lake Reform School, County Monaghan.

Is it possible that Margaret Finn was prostituting herself at this early stage of her young life? In 1890, the average age of a Dublin prostitute was 18 years old. When Margaret Finn arrived back to her family in Dublin, she discovered that her two older sisters, Nannie and Bridget were already involved in prostitution and were well known to the local police. They could very possibly have introduced Margaret to this way of life as a means to an end, as a way of supporting her new born baby.

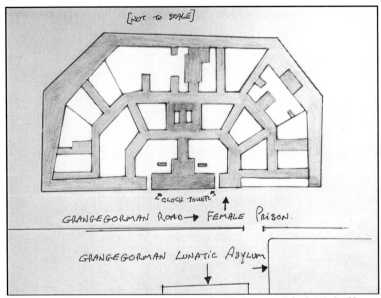

Plan of Grangegorman Female Prison with 256 Cells.

Margaret's older sister, Bridget had married John Nutter but was now a young widow; she was 4 feet 11 inches in height with brown hair and hazel eyes. On the 27th November 1883, 15 year old Bridget Finn, alias Mary Collins from Barrack Street, was sentenced to six months imprisonment in Grangegorman Female Penitentiary for assault. On the 1st July 1887, 19 year old Bridget Finn, alias Mary Robinson, alias Mary Campbell, from Barrack Street was fined twenty shillings for using profane language in a public place. On the 15th January 1894, Huge Boylan, a *'Guinea Man'* was charged with violently assaulting Bridget Nutter at 29 Gloucester Place. Bridget stated that she was speaking to a sick woman in the next room when Boylan came in and accused her of loud talk. He then struck her a punch, threw her down a stairs and kicked her in the stomach.

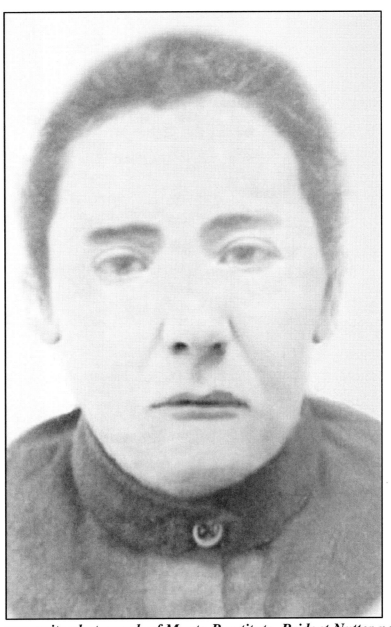

A composite photograph of Monto Prostitute, Bridget Nutter nee Finn, alias Mary Finn, alias Mary Dunne alias Honora Collins alias Bridget Finn. In 1884, 16 year old Bridget Finn alias Florence Campbell was arrested for prostitution. At 15 years of age she was arrested for being drunk.

The next evening as she walked into the hallway of the house where she lived with her mother, the accused approached and assaulted her once again. She then went to the police and reported the assault. Later that evening Boylan again approached her and stabbed her with a knife and then slashed her across the face.

According to the Irish Prison Register, in February of 1901, Bridget Mary Nutter alias Mary Dunne, alias Honora Collins was arrested for being drunk. She was also known to the police as Mary Finn and Bridget Finn, these are just some examples of the many aliases that Bridget would use when arrested for one crime or another.

Over a period of years and on almost every occasion, these three Finn sisters would use many aliases and would swap and change their names to try and confuse the police and the judiciary into thinking they were someone other than who they were and hopefully not give them a very lengthy 'Wrap Sheet'.

In 1900, 36 year old Thomas Wall was sentenced to two months in Mountjoy Jail for assaulting Bridget Nutter. He claimed that she picked his pockets while he was sleeping. In 1903, 32 year old widower, Charlie Snipe who was blind in one eye, was charged with assaulting Bridget Nutter. He claimed she was stealing money from his trouser pocket while he was drunk. In 1904, 22 year old James Wankley was sentenced to eight months in Mountjoy Prison for assaulting Bridget Nutter. He claimed that she robbed him of five shillings.

*By the time they were 20 years of age, many Monto prostitutes
were already seasoned alcoholics.*

Bridget Nutter was battered and bruised over the years and was very unlucky when it came to getting one up on any of her customers. She worked her trade separately from her two sisters, never working the same patch or street as they covered, even though they all worked in the same area. Bridget seems to have been a loner. She had no man to look out for her or offer her any protection from troubled clients. In this respect, she was very different to the other prostitutes in the area. By 1901 Bridget Nutter had reverted back to her maiden name of Finn.

By the time Margaret Finn was 20 years of age she too, was involved in and arrested for prostitution. On the 25th February 1889, 19 year old Margaret was living in Hill Street, Dublin and it was here that she was arrested for being drunk and disorderly. She was sentenced by the court to serve one calendar month in Grangegorman Female Prison; she had come full circle, ending up back where she began her life behind bars. According to her arrest sheet from 1896, 24 year old, Margaret Finn was up before the Judge on at least nine different occasions for drunkenness and assault.

On the 30th of July 1891, Margaret Finn was living with Patrick Carroll, the father of two of her three children, and had changed her name to Margaret Carroll. There is no evidence however, to prove or otherwise disprove, that they may have ever been married.

It was in this year, of 1891, that Margaret gave birth to her second child, Annie Carroll. Two years later, on Christmas Day in 1893, Margaret gave birth to her third child, Christopher Patrick Carroll.

This is the original clock tower and main administration section of Grangegorman Female Prison. Also shown are two of its original wings, on the left pointing east and on the right pointing north.

This is another original wing of the prison pointing north. The section of the building on the left with the downpipe and windows is a part of the prison that extended out at an angle to meet up with the central walkway of cells.

Monto women had it tough, nothing ever came easy.

On the 10th June 1898, while she was in prison, Margaret Carroll received a letter from the Master of the North Dublin Union Hospital in relation to her five year old son, Christopher. The contents of this letter are unknown but may possibly relate to the early death of this child. One may wonder where Patrick Carroll was on the night that this murder took place and where were his children?

In 1915, Margaret was married to Christopher McDonnell. On their marriage certificate Margaret Finn states that she is a Spinster (unmarried). Because she was born in 1870 this would mean that she was 45 years old when this marriage took place. She used her maiden name, Finn for this marriage and not Carroll, the name she used for most of her adult life, two years later however, when she died, she is only 42 years old. Her husband died two weeks before Margaret in February 1917. On the 8th of February of that same year and some years after her final release from prison, with her daughter Annie by her side, next to Mary Vincent, 47 year old Margaret Carroll died from Heart Failure in number 20 Railway Street. On her death certificate it states that Margaret was a *'Room Keeper'*. She was finally laid to rest in an unmarked pauper's grave in Glasnevin Cemetery, Dublin. Throughout her life of prostitution, Margaret Carroll had used any one of at least 10 aliases, whenever she was arrested.

All sorts of shady characters frequented the Monto.

Chapter 7

Room Money

JOHN BYRNE.

Courtroom sketch of John Byrne.

Thirty one year old John Byrne, from Dunne Street was born in the Curragh, County Kildare and is another of the accused, who testified that he was in a room next door when he heard a row outside on the landing between Nannie McLoughlin and Carrie Thompson. He said that he heard McLoughlin shouting at Thompson and demanding more money for the use of her room. He then heard Carrie Thompson telling Nannie McLoughlin that she had given her all of the money that the man had given to her. Byrne said that he then heard a crash and heard Carrie Thompson crying out that she was bleeding. He further said that he heard Thompson running down the stairs. John Byrne then stated that he heard Nannie McLoughlin asking John McKenna for her '*Room Money*'. McKenna replied that he had given Carrie Thompson all the money he had and said that he was going downstairs. Nannie McLoughlin then said '*Yes, after I throw you down*'. John Byrne told the packed courtroom that John McKenna then went downstairs and stood at the front door of the house. Now, according to this sequence of events, John Byrne states that Nannie McLoughlin and Carrie Thompson were standing outside his room at the top of the stairs having their argument and not in the room next door as Carrie Thompson had testified. He also said that it was outside his door that Thompson was hit with the whiskey bottle and that she then ran down the stairs. This statement is almost opposite in content to that of Carrie Thompson's testimony

Carrie Thompson further told the court that Nannie McLoughlin followed John McKenna down the stairs and had threatened to beat his brains out unless he gave her more money. While John McKenna stood talking to Carrie Thompson in the doorway of the brothel, with his back turned to McLoughlin, Nannie McLoughlin struck him a blow from behind with some kind of a weapon, which Thompson said, may have been a poker, and that McKenna immediately fell to the ground. She then started screaming '*Police*' in the hope that someone would run for the police and get help for John McKenna.

On a previous occasion to this statement, Carrie Thompson had told the police that when she awoke after being knocked unconscious by Nannie McLoughlin, she was alone in her room and had no idea where John McKenna was. In another statement she said that while she was standing at the hall door of the brothel she could hear John McKenna getting a beating upstairs and it was at this point that she screamed for the police. Carrie Thompson appears to give several different interpretations of certain events on that fatal night.

She then told the court that John McKenna was taken out to the back of the house by two men, who she later identified as John McLoughlin and John Byrne, where he was beaten even more by at least three of the accused who used a poker and a hatchet type weapon on him. One neighbour said that she heard Carry Thompson screaming for the police and that from her upstairs window she saw Thompson on the street below covered in blood and that her jacket was red. Carrie Thompson also told the court that as she stood in the doorway of the house she could hear Nannie McLoughlin beating the deceased down the stairs with a poker and that was why she screamed for the police. She also saw a weapon shaped like a hatchet being used as well and that's when she began shouting 'Murder'.

Thompson said that all of the accused were beating McKenna out in the back yard. She said that she heard John Byrne say 'Leave him alone' and then heard Nannie McLoughlin say 'I'm not done with him yet'. She said that she heard McLoughlin call for a poker and heard her swearing and saying 'I'll do for him yet'. Nannie

No place to hide in the Moto.

McLoughlin seemed very intent on finishing off John McKenna with a poker. It may be that this ferocious and vicious attitude of hers should have seen her walk to the gallows on a charge of murder for the death of John McKenna. A neighbour said that she saw John McLoughlin and John Byrne and two of the younger women dragging a man out of the hall. She said that she saw Maggie Carroll robbing the man's pockets while Annie Higgins held the light for her.

On one other occasion Carrie Thompson told the court that while she was lying on the floor of the room where Nannie McLoughlin had struck her the blow of the whiskey bottle she could hear chopping noises coming from downstairs and she could also hear whispering. When asked whose voices she heard, she replied *'I could not tell in the dark, the man was out of the room first and then I got stupid'*. When asked if she was awake, she replied that she was asleep.

Another of the neighbours contacted the police at Summerhill Station and told them that there was trouble in Gloucester Lane. Nannie McLoughlin told the two men to throw John McKenna up against the wall across the lane from their house.

© Martin Coffey

Inside the gate of Grangegorman Female Penitentiary.

Gardiner Street tenement house.

John Byrne testified to the court that Nannie and John McLoughlin asked him to help them move the deceased over to a wall across the lane from their house. The men then began to kick the deceased before dragging him further out of the lane to nearby Gloucester Street. As McKenna lay on the ground dying, Maggie Carroll went through his pockets and stole, as well as other items, a pocket watch which the son of the deceased later identified. John McLoughlin had pawned it the next day and a police officer retrieved it from the pawnshop where the clerk told him that John McLoughlin had pawned it.

Thomas Porter who lived in 9 White's Court, off Purdon Street told the court that all of the accused, with the exception of Annie Higgins, called to his house between one and two o'clock on the morning of the incident and bought four bottles of Stout, which Nannie McLoughlin paid for. John Byrne bought some whiskey also. Margaret Carroll and Annie Higgins were each sentenced to five years imprisonment for an almost minor offence, there was no evidence presented to the court to show that they had any part in the actual slaying of John McKenna.

Later in the day the Police arrested John Byrne, who was drunk and asleep in the hallway of the house, number 3 Gloucester Lane. In one of his coat pockets they found a Skeleton Key belonging to the deceased. There were also fresh blood stains on his coat.

The Police Officer further stated that Nannie McLoughlin said to him *'Could this man not have been murdered in the front house and brought out through this hall and brought to the lane'?* This was a

The Monto was never short of Customers.

ploy by McLoughlin to throw the Police off by suggesting that the crime could have happened in a house, 95 Tyrone Street, the house situated at the back of 3 Gloucester Lane. The back boundary wall dividing these two houses had been knocked down to facilitate easy access from one brothel to the other and was used as a quick means of escape by clients, from either premises, when a police raid was in process.

When Margaret Carroll was being arrested she refused to go unless Mrs Higgins was also taken in with her, stating that Higgins had also played a part in the crime. The Constable then arrested Mrs Higgins downstairs. It appears that Margaret Carroll was making sure that if she was being charged for her role in connection with the murder of John McKenna then so was Annie Higgins. Everyone it seems was guilty by association.

With the exception of Mrs Higgins, all of the prisoners were under the influence of drink when arrested. In John McLoughlin's room the Police found the hatchet used to attack the deceased, it had blood on the handle. They also found part of a smoking pipe that belonged to John McKenna. When Nannie McLoughlin was asked about blood stains on her apron she said that they were from a sheep's head that she had bought in Moore Street the day before.

© Martin Coffey

A prostitute sleeping in Purdon Street, 1930's

Prostitutes very often robbed their customers, taking advantage of them while they slept or were drunk.

When John McLoughlin was arrested and charged he replied '*Do what you like*'. The police found blood stains on his cuffs, sleeves and on his trousers. There were also fresh blood stains on his coat.

According to the Irish Prison Registers 1790–1924, Nannie McLoughlin was charged with manslaughter and sentenced to seven years Penal Servitude for her part in this crime. Her sister, Margaret

Carroll was sentenced to five years Penal Servitude as was Annie Higgins. John McLoughlin and John Byrne both received 10 years Penal Servitude for their part in the manslaughter of John McKenna, they were taken to Kilmainham Jail. On the judge's recommendation, Thomas Higgins was found not guilty and set free. As far as the general public and the newspapers were concerned, this was the end of this affair, and justice was seen to be done.

In 1901 the family of murder victim, John McKenna are living in number 2 Henrietta Street. His eldest son, 21 year old Patrick is not mentioned on this census. Two of his daughters, 16 year old Clara and 14 year old Mary are employed as factory workers. According to the census for this year there are seven families, 34 people in all, living in this house.

6. Ellen Maher Cash	48	5	-	-	Bro	-	105	Britain St 31 Liffey St Chann...		
7. Mary Oats	20	5	-	-	Grey Fresh		130	Gramond	Gramond	N
8. Mary Quinn	24	4	11½	-	-	Fair	118	Nicholas St N. D. Union	-
9. Bridget Finn Robinson. Campbell	19	4	11	-	-	-	115	Barrack R St 14 Chancery Bros Lane	
6840 Bridget Fagan	18	5	-	-	Blue Fresh		125	Bolton Court N. D. Union	N

In 1887, 19 year old prostitute, Bridget Finn, alias Bridget Nutter,
alias Florence Campbell, alias Bridget Robinson, alias Mary
Collins was arrested and charged with assault.

An old derelict brothel in Railway Street that was once frequented
by prostitute, Bridget Nutter.

Chapter 8

Life Behind Bars

© Martin Coffey

Grangegorman Female Penitentiary.

© Martin Coffey

Mountjoy Jail.

A set of photographs taken of prisoner B256, Margaret Carroll in Mountjoy Female Prison in 1900.

In 1889, 19 year old Margaret Finn is arrested for being drunk and disorderly. A reference is made on this entry to Sparks Lake Industrial School where she had spent some years and is dated 22nd October 1883.

The Penal Record of Convict, for Prisoner B260, 24 year old Margaret Carroll alias Margaret McLoughlin states that she is single and a mother of two children. She had in fact, three children. Her place of birth is Portarlington and her trade is that of a prostitute. Her address is given as, 3 Gloucester Lane, Dublin. She is capable of reading and writing and is a Roman Catholic.

© National Archives

Description of the prisoner, Margaret Carroll.

While serving time in Grangegorman Female Prison and Mountjoy Jail, Margaret Carroll spent most of her time occupied with knitting and sewing, this is mentioned on her record as being her '*Prison Trade*'. Was she sewing Mail Bags and knitting socks for the British Army? For this work she was granted '*Two Marks*' per day. She was expected to earn a certain amount of Marks each week and these Marks were noted and entered on her Weekly Record of Marks and Gratuities report. When it came time for an early release this record was consulted and because Margaret had fewer Marks than required her release date was moved to one day later than planned. Whenever Margaret was ill in prison she was awarded full marks for her time away from her work.

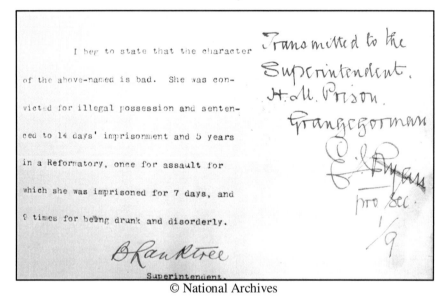

© National Archives

Superintendent's report on Margaret Carroll.

In March of 1898, Margaret Carroll was charged with being insolent to the Prison Matron and as a result was put on a diet of bread and water for 24 hours. In April of that same year she was cautioned for creating a serious disturbance in the laundry room. In November of 1898 she was again in trouble by demanding to be taken to her cell and for making improper remarks to the Prison Officers. For this misbehaviour she was confined to a Punishment

Cell for 48 hours and fed on a diet of bread and water. At another point in time Margaret Carroll was to forfeit Marks representing one week's remission for breaking a pane of glass and a cell stool

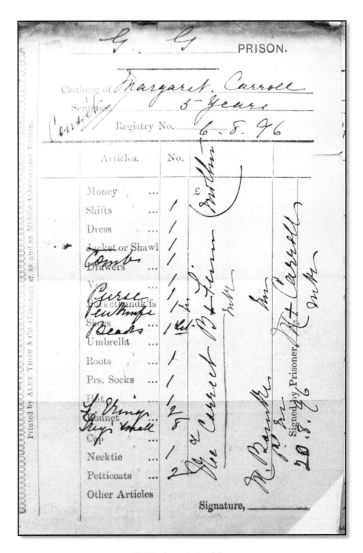

Margaret Carroll's list of personal belongings on entering Grangegorman Female Prison in 1896.

and for disorderly conduct. She was again to be given a diet of bread and water for 24 hours. In November of 1898, Margaret Carroll was placed under restraint in Muffs, this confined the movement of her hands and was also meant to prevent her from doing any injury to herself or to others. She was undergoing 48 hours punishment for insubordination. When the restraint was finally removed it was on the clear understanding that Margaret promised not to *'Misconduct herself again'*.

The prison records show that, on the 27th of April 1897, Margaret Carroll sent a letter to Sister Mary John Evangelist, the Superioress of Saint Francis Industrial School for Girls, in Cashel, County Tipperary. Shortly after her arrest for her part in the manslaughter of John McKenna, Margaret's three children, Joseph Finn, Annie Carroll and Christopher Patrick Carroll were taken into care by the authorities. Eight year old Joseph was sent to the Christian Brothers in Artane Industrial School, Dublin, five year old Annie was sent to the Presentation Sisters in Tipperary and two year old Christopher was sent to the orphanage in the North Dublin Union. Margaret was inquiring about her daughter, Annie's well-being.

On the 1st of May, 1897 Margaret received a letter from her daughter, Annie. There are no copies of the letters Margaret sent or of the ones received, with her prison file; they would have been considered her personal property to keep. Margaret was given each letter on the day it arrived at the prison. In September of that same year Margaret wrote once again to her daughter in Tipperary. The following week she received another reply from Annie.

Cooking over an open fire was very often the only means by which people could make a hot meal for their family. Some of the old tenement houses had no doors leading from the rooms out onto the Landings because they were taken down and used on the fire to cook a dinner.

In June of 1898, Margaret Carroll received a letter from the Master of the North Dublin Union, in relation to her son, Patrick Carroll. This letter was probably to inform Margaret of the death of her youngest child. There is no evidence of Margaret Carroll ever

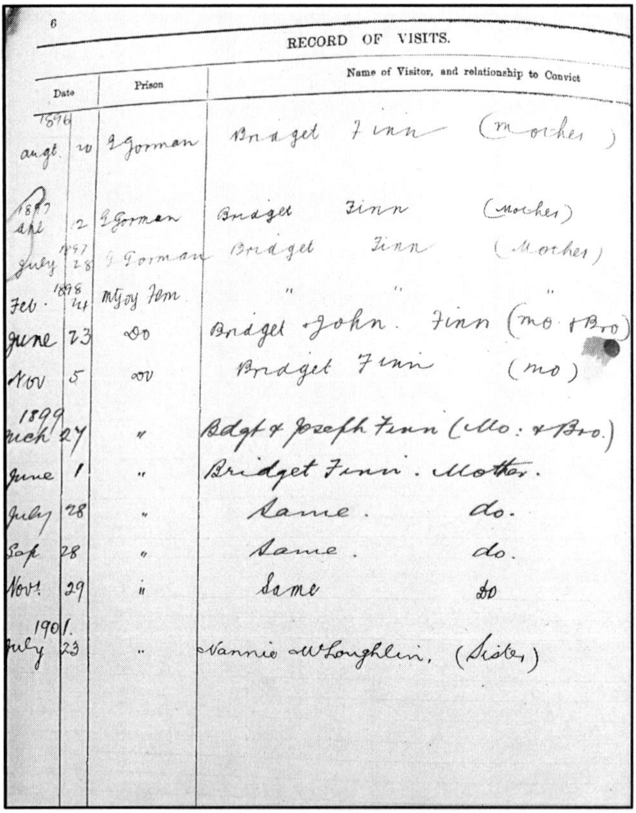

© National Archives

A portion of the 'Record of Visits' showing some of the visitors that came to see Margaret Carroll in both Grangegorman Female Prison and Mountjoy Jail from 1896 to 1901. Interestingly enough, one of those visitors was her sister, Nannie McLoughlin who came to tell Margaret that she was going back to America.

writing to the Christian Brothers in Artane Industrial School inquiring about her son, Joseph or Joe as he was later known. That same year Margaret received another letter from Tipperary. This was probably in relation to her daughter, Annie making her First Holy Communion. Margaret also wrote to her mother from time to time.

110

Writing letters from prison.

When Margaret Carroll was serving time in Grangegorman Women's Prison, her mother was the only family member who paid her any visits there. Her father, Leonard Finn is never mentioned in any visits or correspondence. When Margaret was serving time in Mountjoy Jail, her mother, once again was a regular visitor. On the 23rd June 1898 her mother and a younger brother, John Finn paid her a visit. In March of the following year another brother, Joseph Finn paid her a visit, along with their mother.

In late 1899, a decision was made to grant Margaret Carroll an early release through an Order of Licence, this decision was based on her overall behaviour while in prison and the amount of marks she had accumulated through her work while there. Margaret had to give an undertaking that she would keep out of trouble, stay clear of prostitutes, brothels and Shebeens, stay sober and not associate with anyone of a criminal nature. If she failed to keep to this undertaking her Licence would be revoked and she would return to prison to sit

© National Archives

Maggie Carroll arrested in 1900 for being drunk.

out the remaining time of her original sentence. It was also expected of the prisoner to carry with her at all times, her Licence, as proof to any Policeman or Judge that she was legally out of prison. True to her nature, Margaret was no sooner out of prison when she was arrested, once again for being drunk. On her original release from prison, Margaret Carroll had no option but to return to the address at which she was originally arrested for her part in the manslaughter of John McKenna, she had nowhere else to go. So, straightaway she had broken her early release contract by frequenting a known brothel. Her neighbourhood too was full of known criminals and prostitutes. On her arrest, Margaret was sent to Mountjoy Prison to serve out the remaining time of her original sentence.

On the 23rd of July 1901, Margaret Carroll received a visit from her older sister, Nannie McLoughlin. She too had been given an early release from prison on similar terms to Margaret. Nannie was now widowed and had come to say goodbye to her sister, as she was planning to return to America to live out the remainder of her life. This must have been a very sad occasion for both of these sisters and especially after all that they had been through together.

On the 19th of September 1900, Nannie's husband, John McLoughlin had died insane in Dundrum Mental Asylum in Dublin. She had also learned that, 44 year old Annie Higgins, another of the accused in this murder case, had died in Mountjoy Prison hospital on the 6th of December 1898.

Nothing further is known of what became of John Byrne, who was sentenced to 10 years for his role in the murder. Nannie also discovered that, shortly after the court case, 19 year old Carrie Thompson, the key witness in the murder trial, was attacked in Purdon Street by two women, Kate Allen and Anne Jane Doran, because she *'Turned informer and took the witness stand'*. Carrie had one of her teeth knocked out and was kicked to the ground by her attackers. On the previous night to this attack she was chased down Railway Street by a mob and had to run into a Police Station for protection. No more is known of whatever became of Carrie Thompson.

On the 22nd of January 1901, Queen Victoria of England died and her son, Prince Albert took over the throne as Edward VII, King of the United Kingdom and the British Dominions and Emperor of

In 1901, King Edward VII of England granted an early prison release to sisters, Margaret Carroll and Nannie McLoughlin. He was said to be a regular visitor to the Monto when he did his military training in the Curragh Army Camp in County Kildare. He would use the Monto's underground tunnels to sneak in and out unnoticed.

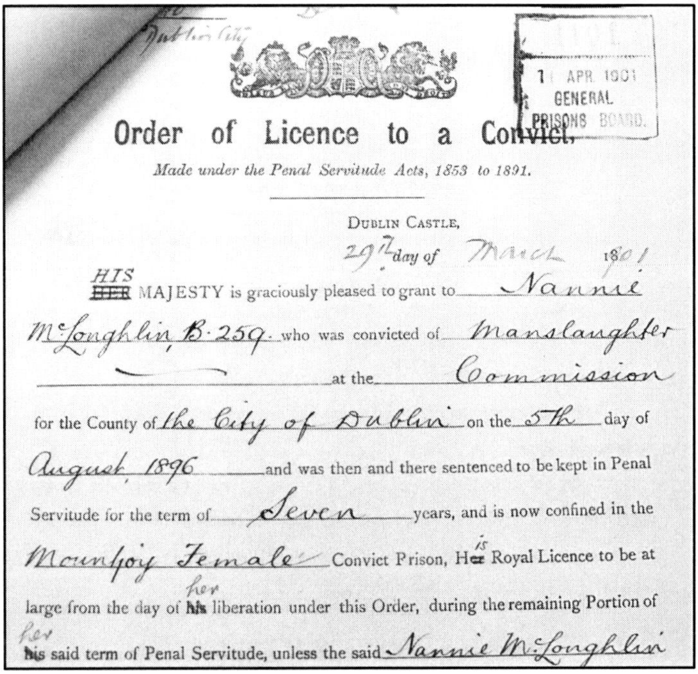

Dublin City

1 APR 1901
GENERAL
PRISONS BOARD.

Order of Licence to a Convict.

Made under the Penal Servitude Acts, 1853 to 1891.

DUBLIN CASTLE,

29th day of March 1901

~~HER~~ HIS MAJESTY is graciously pleased to grant to Nannie McLoughlin, B·259 who was convicted of Manslaughter at the Commission for the County of the City of Dublin on the 5th day of August, 1896 and was then and there sentenced to be kept in Penal Servitude for the term of Seven years, and is now confined in the Mountjoy Female Convict Prison, ~~Her~~ His Royal Licence to be at large from the day of ~~his~~ her liberation under this Order, during the remaining Portion of ~~his~~ her said term of Penal Servitude, unless the said Nannie McLoughlin

© National Archives

'Order of Licence' for Nannie McLoughlin.

(Should space for further visits be required, a sheet of foolscap paper ruled as above to be inserted.)

DISPOSAL ON RELEASE.

Date			Whether on Licence, Pardon, Remission or Expiration of Sentence or Death, &c.	Licence Number	Remanet		Destination
Day	Month	Year			Years	Days	
5	12	99	On Licence which will expire on 3rd Aug 1901	24 Dublin City	1	241	No 96½ Tyrone St Dublin
8	9	01	On 2nd Licence of 191 Days which will expire on 18th March 02	14 Dublin City	-	191	32 Mabbott Pl, Dublin.

© National Archives

Margaret Carroll was released from prison on Licence in 1899. This was later revoked due to her being drunk but was issued a second time in 1901.

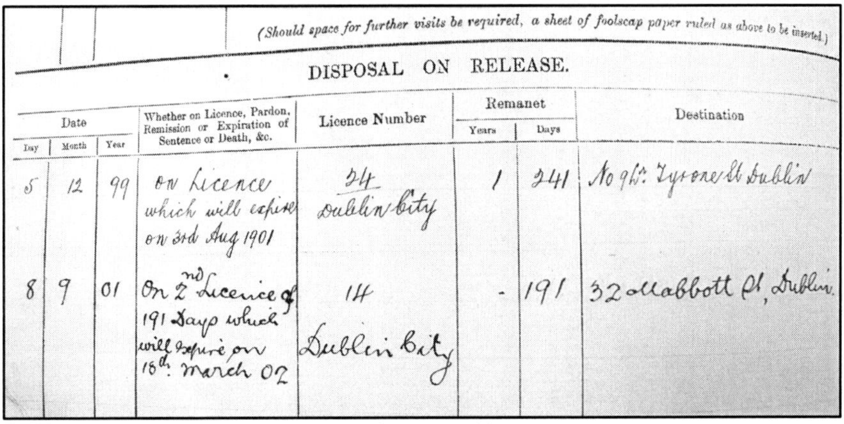

India. Whenever a new King or Queen took over the British Throne they would very often grant an early release for a certain category of prisoner throughout their kingdom and dominions and it seems most likely that this is why Nannie McLoughlin and Margaret Carroll were granted an *'Order of Licence'* in March of 1901

© Martin Coffey

Margaret Carroll died in number 20 Railway Street.

When Margaret Carroll was eventually released from Mountjoy Jail, she went to live in 27 Hill Street, Dublin. She was safe from further arrest as this address was situated outside the boundary of the Monto. In 1902 and with failing sight, Margaret Carroll is once again arrested on a charge of drunkenness but is let off with a fine of five shillings. From this date on there is no mention of Margaret on any police arrest sheet or court record.

On the 8th of February 1917, 47 year old Margaret Carroll nee Finn died in her room at 20 Railway Street, in Dublin's Monto District, twenty one years after the death of John McKenna. For almost 30 years she had plied her trade as a Prostitute. She had seen the inside of an Industrial School, Police Stations and Prison Cells and had become a young mother long before she reached her 21st birthday. Was there ever any hope of a different life on offer to her or was she too, a victim of circumstances?

© National Archives

On an arrest charge for being drunk in 1902, Margaret Carroll gives her surname as Brady. In Grangegorman and Mountjoy Prisons she spent most of her time knitting and sewing.

117

Within months of being re-united with her daughter, after an absence of almost 15 years, 47 year old Margaret Carroll died on the 8th of February 1917.

Chapter 9

Nannie McLoughlin

© National Archives

Prisoner B259, Monto Madam, 30 year old, Nannie McLoughlin nee Finn, at the time of her imprisonment in Grangegorman Female Penitentiary in1896. Nannie is a sister to Margaret Carroll.

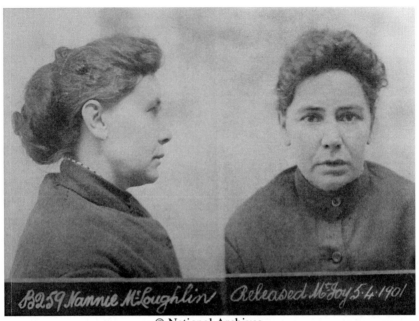

© National Archives

A set of photographs taken of prisoner B250, Nannie McLoughlin in Mountjoy Female Prison in 1901.

2057		3781	Ellen Coyle	21	5	5½	Br Blu	,,			142 143	Dundalk	Dundalk	Pros
3080 18	5	2	Lucy Glynn Farnan O'Toole	21	5	0½	Br Br	,,			110	James St	2 Duffers St	Dealer
2112-90	31	3	Cath Murphy Mary Kelly Gilson	49	5	0	Br Br	Sal	,,		124	Drogheda	9 Cook St	,,
266 90 until 738 - CR	X 13	4	Anne McLoughlin O'Loughlin Mack McLoud	24	5	2¾	,,	Gy fresh			116	Barrack St	3 Gloster Lane	Pros X
2159	1	38	5	Sarah Kearney Gallagher Hogarty Ireland	31	5	1	,,	,,	,,	cut on nose	120	Meath St	117 Cork St	,,
2049	18	6	Mary A Walsh Daly	30	5	0	,,	Blu	,,		139	Thos St	117 do	,,
2972	18	7	Mary Coleman Lilly Beure Kergan Tyrrell	21	4	10	,,	Br	,,		118	Sandwith St	16 Ross Lane	Pros

In 1900 Nannie McLoughlin was arrested for being drunk. Her address is given as, 3 Gloucester Lane. Her profession is stated as that of a Prostitute.

On her Penal Record of Conviction, 30 year old Nannie McLoughlin states that she was born in Barrack Street, Dublin, She was in fact born, Anne Finn in Portarlington in 1862. The record states that her husband, John is serving a ten year sentence in Mountjoy Prison. Nannie's trade is given as that of a prostitute. At the time of her arrest she was living in number 3 Gloucester Lane. The record says that Nannie is illiterate, that she is unable to read or write. Like her sister, her *'Prison Trade'* was knitting and sewing. Over the years Nannie had already spent time in both Grangegorman Female Prison and Mountjoy Jail for various offences ranging from drunkenness to assault, to prostitution and stealing.

Two for the price of one in the Monto?

121

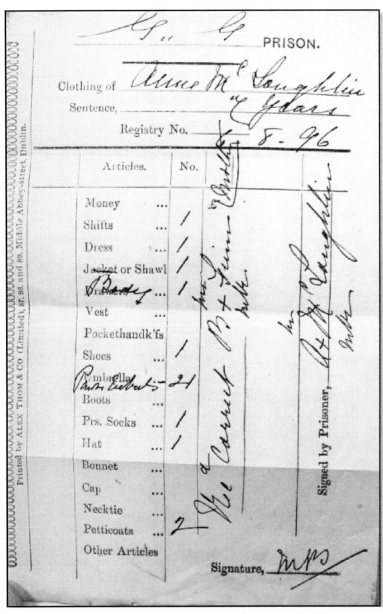

© National Archives

A list of items belonging to Nannie McLoughlin on admission to Grangegorman Prison in 1896, including 21 Pawn Tickets. Nannie signed her name with an X.

© National Archives

Penal Record of Convict B259, Nannie McLoughlin.

On the 22nd of November 1898, a letter written by Nannie
McLoughlin and sent to her husband, John McLoughlin in
Maryborough Prison, Portlaoise, was returned to her. It was then
forwarded to Dundrum Mental Asylum. On the 22nd of December
1900, Nannie McLoughlin sent a letter to her sister, Bridget Nutter
at number 9 White's Court but the letter was returned undelivered,
with a note saying *'Not known at this address'*. In January of 1901,
the Prison Governor of Mountjoy Jail received a request from the
Governor of Maryborough Prison, inquiring about the discharge

date of Nannie McLoughlin. He wanted to send her, her late husband's *'Prison Gratuity'*. John McLoughlin was deemed to be insane and was sent to Dundrum Mental Asylum in Dublin, where he later died. For his role in the killing of John McKenna, McLoughlin was originally sent to Kilmainham Jail to serve out his sentence. It seems however, that at some stage of his prison life, he was moved from here and sent to Mountjoy Jail and then on to Maryborough Prison in Portlaoise.

It would seem by all accounts that Nannie McLoughlin, unlike her sister Margaret behaved herself while in prison. There are few negative comments or entries on her prison record. On the 19th of January, 1899 there is an entry on Nannie's record in relation to an application to the Lord Lieutenant and to the Governor of the Prison asking for Nannie's sentence to be reduced, *'To even 5 year'*. One week later she got her answer, *'The law must take its course'*.

In this petition Nannie states that she is innocent of the charge of manslaughter and blames her condition at the time of the murder on drink. It is interesting too that at this stage she talks about her planned return trip to America whenever she is released from prison.

Prisoner B 259 Nannie McLoughlin 19th January 1899

That petitioner was tried on the 5th day of August 1896 at Green Street court on a charge of manslaughter and sentenced to seven years penal servitude. That petitioner most respectfully begs leave to state she is innocent of the crime she is charged with, she petitions being under the influence of drink at the time the deed was committed and has no recollection of ever seeing the man until she saw him dead. She is a young woman and intends, when she leaves prison, to emigrate to a foreign country where she is willing to earn an honest livelihood for herself. She is now going on two and a half years in prison. She therefore most earnestly implores your Excellency to be graciously pleased to extend to her your prerogative of mercy and in your kind consideration be pleased to reduce her sentence, even to five years and your petitioner is in duty bound, will ever pray.

Nannie McLoughlin

In this second petition Nannie McLoughlin once again states her innocence and decides to play the sympathy card in relation to her husband's incarceration in a mental asylum and his impending demise. She also brings God into the equation in an attempt to win over the Lord Lieutenant.

Prisoner B 259 Nannie McLoughlin 3rd of October 1899

That petitioner was tried on the 5th day of August 1896 at Green Street court on a charge of manslaughter and sentenced to seven years penal servitude. She begs most respectfully to state she is not guilty of the offence. Her husband, who was charged with her and others with the above crime was sentenced to ten years penal servitude and is now an inmate of the Dundrum Lunatic Asylum, is in a very delicate state of health and is, she has been informed, getting weaker every day. Her punishment is a very severe one now that her husband is about to be taken from her, but she feels that she deserves it all for having led such a careless and intemperate *life as it was owing to the vices of drunkedness on the part of herself and others concerned in the above offence and not through any intended violence, that the poor man lost his life. She sees now the misery her life of drunkedness has brought on her and is resolved, with the assistance of God, to lead a temperate one for the future and make atonement for the past. The petitioner is in a most depressed state of mind thinking of her poor insane husband. She most humbly implores of your Excellency to be gratefully pleased to take the circumstances of her sad case into your merciful consideration and grant her the mitigation of the remainder of her sentence, that she may have the consolation of seeing her husband before he dies and she, as in duty bound, will ever pray.*

Nannie McLoughlin.

Nannie's request is denied, the reply from the Lord Lieutenant's office states, *'The law must take its course'*. Once again her plea for leniency fell on deaf ears. In relation to this request, there was also a note on this file from the Police Superintendent, which reads as follows, *'I beg to state that the above named woman, Nannie McLoughlin, is a woman of bad character who was previously convicted for assaults, she was arrested on charges of larceny and drunkenness, soliciting and other minor offences'.*

On the 6th October 1899 a note was entered on Nannie McLoughlin's file, *'Her husband is in a weak condition and is losing strength every day. The convict states that she is in a most depressed state of mind. The prison doctors state that she is not suffering from mental depression'.*

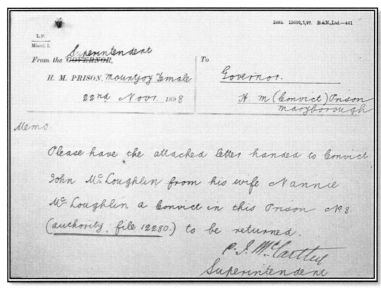

Written onto Nannie McLoughlin's prison record and dated the 22nd November 1898, is this note relating to a letter she had sent to her husband, John who was serving a part of his 10 year sentence in Maryborough Prison, Portlaoise.

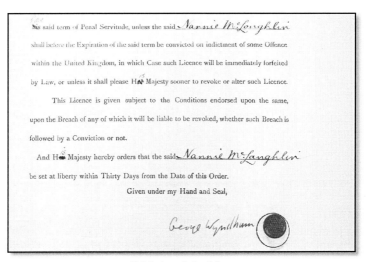

On the 29th of March 1901, Prisoner B259, Nannie McLoughlin is granted a licence of freedom.

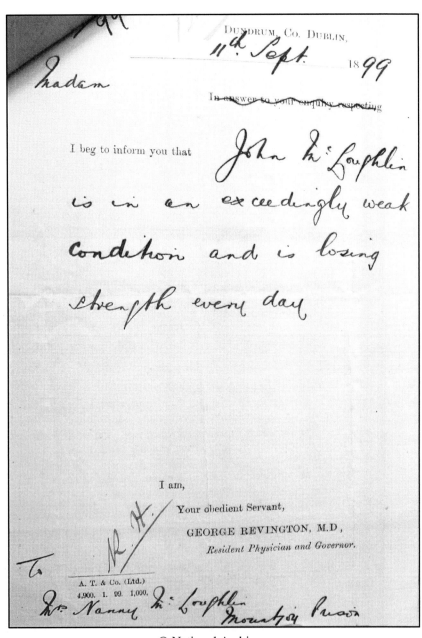

Letter to Nannie McLoughlin from Dundrum Mental Asylum in 1899, informing her of her husband's mental and physical condition.

A Monto couple in Beaver Street with a chicken strolling along in the background.

When Nannie McLoughlin was first admitted into Grangegorman Female Prison and under '*Convict Prison Rules*' the Prison Medical Officer stated that Nannie was considered fit for '*Restraint by Handcuffs, Waist Belt and Muffs, Loose Restraint Jacket, Ankle Straps or Straight Jacket*'. She was also seen as fit, if necessary, to receive punishment in any of the following ways, '*Close Confinement, Separate Confinement, Number 1 Scale Punishment Diet, Number 2 Scale Punishment Diet, Depravation of Mattress*'.

In December of 1900, Nannie McLoughlin was transferred to the Prison Hospital, suffering from stricture of the urethra and the removal of small cancerous growths, for which she had to undergo a very serious operation. She was therefore exempted from any prison work for a period of time. On the 11th of January 1901, the Prison Superintendent wrote to the Medical Officer, wanting to know if the prisoner, '*Having being exempted from labour*' was entitled to full

Marks for that period. These are Marks earned for work carried out by Nannie in her knitting and sewing time. The Marks were granted. She was then put on a special diet of one pound of beef, liver of mutton, two ounces of butter and one pint of milk and soda water.

© National Archives

In January of 1898, Nannie McLoughlin's mother sent her a message on a scrap of paper, telling her that Patrick Curden is in perfect health.

On the 21st of March 1901, Prison Superintendent, C.J. McCarthy wrote to the Chairman of the General Prisoners Board in Dublin Castle, with a submission on behalf of Nannie McLoughlin, asking for special consideration in relation to her upcoming *'Release on Licence'*. He states that Nannie will have the required number of Marks earned under a seven years sentence of Penal Servitude, with one Mark left over, if her conduct and industry continue very satisfactorily. Nannie McLoughlin's prison record also contained a newspaper clipping of her trial, outlining the story of what had occurred and the outcome of the trial.

Although Nannie McLoughlin, in general, kept her head down and did her knitting and sewing and spent time in quiet solitude, there were two occasions when she found herself in trouble within the prison system. On the 20th of September, 1896, she was put on a diet of bread and water for talking in the Prison Chapel. On the 19th of January 1900, she refused to work in a store, for this Nannie was locked up in her own cell for 24 hours and once again fed a diet of bread and water. Nannie received the occasional visits from her mother and her younger brother, John.

> I beg to state that the above-named is a woman of bad character who was previously convicted four times for assaults, and fourteen times for minor offences.
>
> *B Rauktree*
>
> Superintendent.

Remarks regarding the character of Nannie McLoughlin in September of 1896.

© Martin Coffey

In the late 19th century, Elliott Place and Faithful Place were over-run with Prostitutes and Shebeens.

According to the prison record for McLoughlin, she was released *'On Licence'* on the 5th of April 1901. The agreement that Nannie had to undertake meant that, similar to her sister Margaret, she had to stay clear of all trouble, drink, prostitution and keep out of the Monto or she would find herself back behind bars. Her Licence was due to expire in 1903. If she still had a clean slate by then she would not be taken back into prison to serve out the remainder of her original sentence. Throughout her life of prostitution and Shebeening, Nanny used any one of 17 different aliases whenever she was arrested.

Did Nannie McLoughlin ever show any remorse for her actions that led to the death of John McKenna; did she give any thought for his wife and children? And whatever became of Nannie in later years?

On her release from prison, Nannie McLoughlin was now widowed, single and free. She also had money due to her from her husband's time in prison. Nannie lived for a short while with her parents before coming to a decision, which she had made while in prison, to change her name back to Finn and to return to America.

Within a relatively short time after her release from prison, Nannie McLoughlin sailed to America for a fresh start in life. She settled for some time in Mamaroneck Village, Westchester, New York where she was once again employed as a Domestic Servant. She was then known as Mary Finn and had changed her age, instead of being 40 years old; she claimed she was 33. Nannie also stated that she was living in America since 1886; she mentions nothing of her return visit to Ireland or her prison sentence. This is another example of Annie being economical with the truth. Supposedly, old habits die hard and this certainly seems to have been the case with Nannie McLoughlin. In 1902, Mamaroneck was a farming community located on both sides of the Mamaroneck River, overlooking Long Island Sound.

Monto customers were very often 'Short-Changed' by the prostitutes and their strong-armed men and especially if they were enticed into the 'Man-Trap'.

1901 New York census showing Nannie McLoughlin's change of name to Mary Finn.

At one time it was the location of summer residences for wealthy families from New York City and it may have been one of these families that Nanny worked for. Some years later and for reasons unknown, Nannie McLoughlin alias Mary Finn moved to Ontario, Canada and re-married to George Frank Jarrett on the 31st May 1917

Canadian Marriage certificate for Annie Marshall in 1917.

Is it possible that Annie Marshall, the woman named on this marriage certificate from Ontario, Canada in 1917 is actually Nannie McLoughlin alias Mary Finn? On this certificate her mother is named as Bridget Foster. She gives her father's name as John McLocklin (*Loughlin*); this is the name of Nannie's deceased husband back in Ireland. Her age is given as 46 years; she was actually 56 years old. The name of the husband on this certificate is given as George Frank Jarrett, the same name as Nannie McLoughlin's second husband.

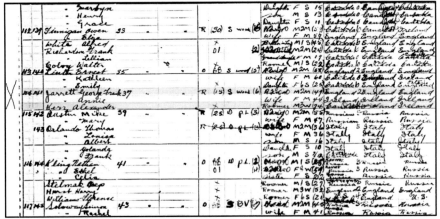

Toronto 1921 census.

On the 1921 census for Toronto, Canada, it shows 49 year old George Frank Jarrett; he is employed as a Fireman in a factory. His 44 year old wife, Annie, is a Catholic who was born in Ireland. They have a 74 year old, Kerr Alexander from Ireland living with them. His occupation is given as that of a Night Watchman in a factory. Was George Jarrett ever made aware of his new wife's shady past and prison life back in Dublin, Ireland?

136

On the 27th of January, 1932, 70 year old Nannie McLoughlin died in Saint Michael's Hospital under the name of Annie Jarrett and she was buried in Saint-Catherine's Cemetery, Niagara Regional Municipality, Ontario, Canada. Her home address is given as 118 Eastern Avenue, York, Ontario, Canada and she had lived there for 25 years. She died from Acute Pneumonia. On her death certificate it mentions her parents as Leonard Finn and Bridget Foster from Ireland. She also had her correct age on the certificate. Nannie is buried in Mount Hope Cemetery.

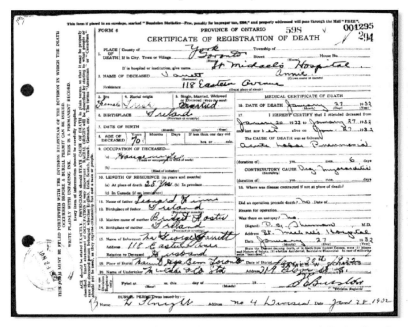

York, Toronto, Canada, 1932, Nannie McLoughlin's death certificate. Her parents are named as Leonard Finn and Bridget Foster from Ireland.

Did Nannie McLoughlin ever keep in touch with her family back in Ireland and especially her sister, Margaret Carroll? Or did she cut off her past and leave it all behind when she stepped onto the boat for America? Nannie eventually died a long way away from her young life in Dublin's Monto District and even further away from *'The Hangman's Noose'*, which she managed to dodge all those years ago.

The final resting place of Nannie McLoughlin, former prostitute from 'The Monto' in Dublin, Ireland.

Chapter 10

John McLoughlin

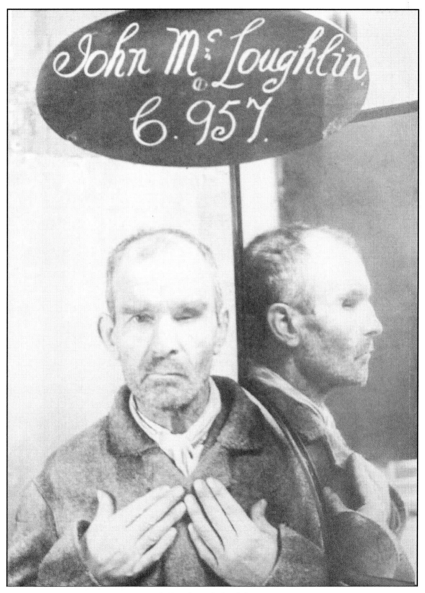

© National Archives

Prison photograph of Convict C 957, John McLoughlin, 1896.

John McLoughlin was a very nasty piece of work, a vicious thug who was no stranger to violence and had spent time in and out of prison. At 14 years of age he was arrested for being drunk in a public place. But as time went by he became more aggressive and vicious in his behaviour. Two years later, in 1867 he is given a two months prison sentence on a charge of assault. At 18 years of age he is before the court on charges of assault, wounding, larceny and burglary, for this he is sentenced to nine months in Kilmainham Gaol.

In 1879 he spends five more days in prison for being drunk. In 1871 he is up on a charge of maliciously wounding Ellen Higgins, a young prostitute and is sentenced to six months in prison. In 1873 he is back in court once again on a charge of aggravated assault on a female, for which he gets a sentence of six months. In 1874 he is charged with *"Larceny from a person"*. This time the judiciary hand down a much tougher sentence and put him away for five years penal servitude. He was originally sent to Mountjoy Prison but was then transferred to Spike Island in County Cork. This Island was at one time used to house prisoners awaiting transportation to the British Penal Colonies. From here, John McLoughlin was transferred to Lusk Prison in County Dublin.

Lusk was known as an *'Intermediate Prison'* where the aim was to establish an environment in which the prisoner *was 'Assailed by temptations'* and his conduct as a reformed person was put on trial. Prisoners were usually employed outside of the prison and were sometimes sent to visit shops as a test of self-discipline. They were

'Take that, yeah robber'.

required to save most of their earnings so that they would have a reasonable amount of money when discharged. The prison authorities looked on this type of *'Intermediate Prison'* as a sort of finishing school for offenders.

Shortly after his release from here however, John McLoughlin is arrested for an assault on another young prostitute. In 1893 he spends two months back in Mountjoy Gaol for assaulting two more prostitutes. At this stage in his life he is married to a *'Brothel Madam'* named Nanny Finn and is working as her *'Enforcer'*. The two prostitutes he recently beat up were probably working for her and when they stepped out of line he was told to teach them a lesson.

KNOWN PARTICULARS OF FORMER CONVICTIONS

No. of former Convictions	Offences for which previously Convicted.	No. of times in Penal Servitude.	Former Prison Character.	
14.	Burglary. Malicious assault to inflict bodily harm. Assaults. Illegal possession Fighting. Drunkenness.+ Disorderly.	once.	Good.	

STAGES IN CLASSIFICATION.

Probation Class. (60 Marks.)	Fourth Class. (120 Marks.)	Third Class. (180 Marks.)	Second Class. (360 Marks.)	
From 5.8 1896	From	From	From	Fr
To 12.8 1896	To	To	To	

John McLoughlin's past history.

A courtroom sketch of John McLoughlin from 1896.

A newspaper from 1893, reports that 19 year old Leonard Finn, a Shoemaker and younger brother of Nannie (Finn) McLoughlin, was arrested for beating up John McLoughlin and kicking him about the head. Perhaps McLoughlin had beat up on his wife and her brother took it on himself to teach McLoughlin a lesson. On his prison file in 1896 a description is given of 45 year old Convict C 957, John McLoughlin. His hair is already turning grey and he is five feet, five and a half inches in height. One of the main features of McLoughlin however, is that he had only one eye, the right one. There is no information available to account for the loss of his left eye but he may have lost this in a knife fight. This lack of an eye,

Place	Court	Date			Christian Name	Surname	Crime	Sentence
		Day	Month	Year				

Statement shewing date of Reception, and Trade followed at each Prison.

Prison	Date			Trade or Occupation	Signature of Governor or Officer in Charge
	Day	Month	Year		
Mountjoy Local	5	8	96	Picking rope junk	_Jos. Meehan(?)_
Mountjoy Convict	12	8	96	Brushmaking Winding yarn matmaking Labourer	_do_
"					"
Maryboro	28	12	97		_J. Bourke(?) Governor_
Dundrum Asylum	7	1	99		

(This Document is not to be folded.)

© National Archives

Time spent in prison.

in itself, would have given him a nasty look to suit his temper. At some point in his life, John McLoughlin had been involved in a very serious and dangerous knife-fight as he had a deep cut mark on his left cheek. There were also cut marks on the bridge of his nose, cut marks over his right eyebrow and several cut marks on his forehead. He had cut marks on the back of his left hand near to his wrist and he also had a cut mark on the back of his head.

This is the kind of man that John McLoughlin had become and he had no hesitation in using these skills on anyone who stood in his way and this included the victim, John McKenna. As part of his sentence in prison, John McLoughlin was required to work. In Mountjoy Prison in 1896 he was set to work at picking Rope Junk for use on ships, Brush Making and Mat Making. When he was later transferred to Maryborough Prison in Portlaoise he was confined to the Labourer section. According to his police records, John McLoughlin never did an honest day's work and so being forced to do so, at this late stage of his life would not have gone down well with him. When imprisoned for manslaughter in 1896, McLoughlin requested that his civilian clothing be given to his niece, Kate McLoughlin.

The monotonous life of day to day drudgery making brushes and mats must have played havoc with McLoughlin and in particular the job of picking and pulling small lengths of rope apart would certainly not go down too well with this *'Street Thug'*. When he was transferred to Maryboro Prison he was assigned to do labouring work and this is certainly something that he would have shied away from all his life. John McLoughlin did not like being told what to do.

Deadlier than the Male.

	OUT-GOING LETTERS.			IN-COMING LETTERS.			
DATE WHEN WRITTEN	ADDRESS OF LETTER	Letters in Supers Master.	NAME AND ADDRESS OF WRITER	WHEN RECEIVED	WHEN ISSUED	Issues of MEDICAL OFFICER	

RECORD of Letters written and received by *John McLoughlin* C.957

19.2.97	Mrs. Nannie McLoughlin (wife) Grangegorman Prison Board's Sanction) ⁵⁴/₂²¹	JW	From Nannie McLoughlin (wife) Grangegorman Prison (Board's Sanction)	13.2.97	15.2.97	JW
			From do. do	17.8.97	18.8.97	JW
20.5.98	To Do. Do. Mountjoy Female Prison	JB	To do do Board's sanction	11.6.98	11.6.98	JB
			From Do. Do Board's Sanction File 12280/98	23.11.98	23.11.98	JB

© National Archives

In 1897 John McLoughlin sent a letter from Maryboro Prison to his wife in Mountjoy Prison, she wrote two letters in return. There is no more correspondence between them until almost a year later, in 1898 when he writes to her and once again she replies with two letters. There is nothing on his prison file to indicate what was said in their letters to each other.

MEDICAL HISTORY SHEET.

(To be kept by the Medical Officer, and forwarded with the Prisoner on his removal.)

The Particulars required below must be entered within a Week after the Convict's reception.

General Reg. No. C.957
Name, John McLoughlin   Age on Conviction, 45 Yrs. Mo.
Place of Birth, Clontarf   County, Dublin
Last Place of Abode, 3 Gloucester Lane   County of City of Dublin
Crime, Manslaughter   Sentence, 10 Yrs P.S.
Dates of ..... { Committal, 13.7.96 / Conviction, 5.8.96 }
Number of { Penal Servitude, Once
former Sentences, { Shorter Sentences, Sixteen
General Health previous to present imprisonment, and special maladies from which the Prisoner states he has suffered, } Fair, Left eye lost, right eye weak

© National Archives

146

RECORD of Petitions to Lord Lieutenant, and of Applications by Prisoner *C. 957*
John McLoughlin to the General Prisons Board, or to the Governor

Date.	Statement of Application by the Prisoner.	Reply.
29·2·97 5/22	Submitting for authority to forward a letter to wife in Grangegorman Prison	This letter may be forwarded (sd) J.S.S 22/2/97
10·10·98.	Asks to be let out on the works	Was taken off the works by med. officer (sd) P.J.J 10·10·98.
8: 11. 98.	Asks for change of diet.	No reason for change (sd) Sw 8 Nov. 98
30:12: 98.	Wants to be transferred to Mountjoy as he is not getting his health here.	Referred to Dr Woodhouse (sd). Jan. 30:12.98

© National Archives

On the 5th of October 1898 while working in the Labour section of Maryboro Prison, John McLoughlin begins to complain of Vertigo and is reported as becoming melancholy. His health is not great and he spends most of his time crying and wishing he was dead, even to the extent that if given the opportunity, he says that he would take his own life. This is the beginning of the end for McLoughlin as he slowly but surely slips into a world of insanity. His memory is failing and he begins to become erratic in his behaviour, requesting a change of diet from brown bread to white bread, potatoes one day and none the next day, sleeping badly, eating very little and losing the sight in his right eye. He is constantly complaining of pains in his legs and he is suffering from diarrhea. The medical team are becoming concerned and at this point, they have transferred him to the Invalid Unit of the prison where they can keep a close eye on his daily performance.

A note from the Chief Medical Officer to the Prison Governor reads as follows; *'I respectfully beg to report that convict, C 957, John McLoughlin seems to me to be very much tossed in his mind. He told me today that he would sooner be in Hell than be in this "Dog's Home" and that he would put an end to himself if he got a chance. On last Saturday at exercise he made use of similar expressions. He said he was the best man in Maryboro and to be locked up in a cell and not be allowed out on the works was something he could not understand. He is now in an Observation Cell under special surveillance'*

Another note from the Chief Medical Officer states; *'I respectfully beg to report that convict, C 957, John McLoughlin appears to be most eccentric in his habits for some time past. He makes most rambling statements about his clothing, saying that they do not fit him and requests changes almost every day, though when his clothes were actually changed, he would say they fitted and suited him while the next day saying they were entirely wrong. Also the new books which he never had in his possession before he states in a day or so that he read them before. He says that the Doctor never visits him even though he is seen on a daily basis'.*

On the 4th of January 1899 a medical report certified that; *"Convict C 957 John McLoughlin is insane. I beg to submit the annexed report in duplicate from Doctor W.G. Jacob and the prison*

Life threatening situations very often arose in the Monto when 'Clients' realised that their pockets had been picked or they were short changed in some way or other and especially when alcohol was involved.

Medical Officer, certifying that John McLoughlin has become insane. The original rule of court will be required in order that a copy may be taken from it and sent to the Asylum with the convict". An application was made to the Prison Governor of Maryboro Prison for permission to transfer John McLoughlin to the Mental Asylum in Dundrum, County Dublin. On the 7th of January 1899, John McLoughlin was transferred to Dundrum. Almost two years after his transfer to the asylum in Dublin, John McLoughlin died insane.

© National Archives

'Medical condition probably incurable'.

Maryboro

7 January 1879

I beg to report that
convict 6957 John McLoughlin
was removed this day to
the Central Asylum Dundrum.

Penal Record, Original
Rule of Court. Medical
History Sheet and file.
are returned herewith,

B. Murphy
fur Governor. Lieut.

A gratuity of 18 shillings and 6 pennies are to be paid to the widow of Convict C 957 John McLoughlin, who died insane, in Dundrum Mental Asylum on the 19thof September 1900.

Chapter 11

Anne Higgins

© National Archives

Prisoner B 261, Anne Higgins in her prison garb and bonnet, arms folded to show her hands are not deformed and a mirror used for her profile picture.

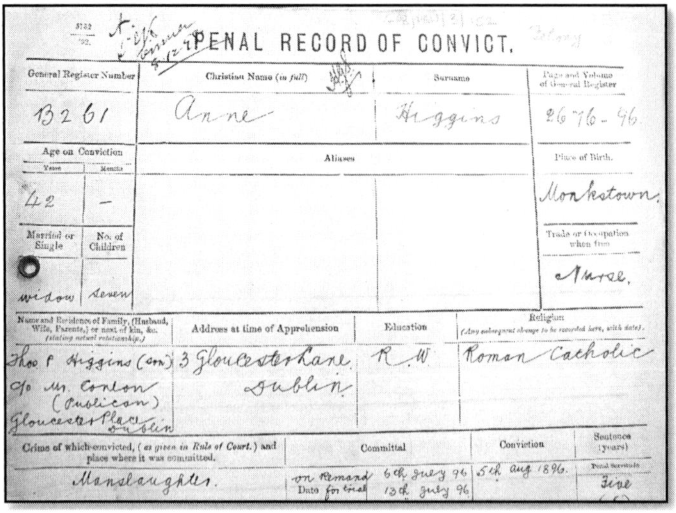

PENAL RECORD OF CONVICT.

General Register Number	Christian Name (in full)	Surname	Page and Volume of General Register
B 261	Anne	Higgins	2676 - 96

Age on Conviction (Years)	Months	Aliases	Place of Birth
42	—		Monkstown

Married or Single	No. of Children	Trade or Occupation when free
widow	seven	Nurse

Name and Residence of Family, (Husband, Wife, Parents,) or next of kin, &c. (stating actual relationship.)	Address at time of Apprehension	Education	Religion (Any subsequent change to be recorded here, with date.)
Thos P. Higgins (son) c/o Mr. Conlon (Publican) Gloucester Place Dublin	3 Gloucester Lane, Dublin	R. W.	Roman Catholic

Crime of which convicted, (as given in Rule of Court.) and place where it was committed.	Committal	Conviction	Sentence (years) Penal Servitude
Manslaughter.	on Remand 6th July 96; Date for trial 13th July 96	5th Aug 1896.	Five

© National Archives

Penal Record of convict B 261, Anne Higgins.

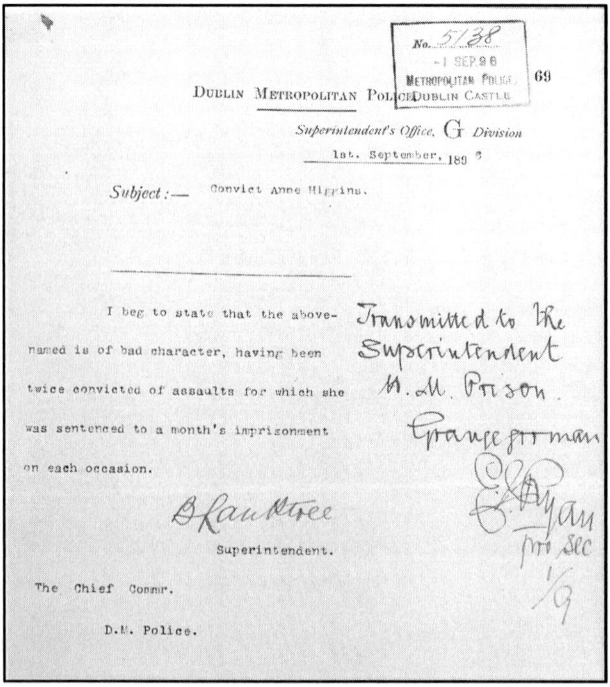

No. 5138
-1 SEP. 96
METROPOLITAN POLICE, DUBLIN CASTLE

69

DUBLIN METROPOLITAN POLICE.

Superintendent's Office, G *Division*

1st. September, 1896

Subject:— Convict Anne Higgins.

I beg to state that the above-named is of bad character, having been twice convicted of assaults for which she was sentenced to a month's imprisonment on each occasion.

B Rowntree

Superintendent.

The Chief Commr.

D.M. Police.

Transmitted to the Superintendent H.M. Prison Grangegorman

E. Ryan
pro Sec
1/9

© National Archives

Anne Higgins, a bad character.

This is a list of clothing worn by Anne Higgins on her arrival in Grangegorman Female Penitentiary in 1896. A prison rule dictated that each prisoner must wear prison clothes only. Anne's usual clothing was given to Bridget Finn, mother of Nannie McLoughlin and Margaret Carroll, for safe keeping.

Anne Higgins was a 42 year old widowed woman with seven children. According to her arrest sheet she was a qualified nurse who was born in Monkstown, County Dublin. Her eldest child was a son, of whom she stated was the bread-winner of the family and he was the one who looked after the rest of his siblings while their mother was in prison. Unfortunately and according to Anne, this son had died since her arrest and imprisonment. This may be the son; Thomas P. Higgins who was also arrested in connection with the murder of John McKenna but was later acquitted. Anne gives no indication as to whose care the rest of her children were in since her son's death. Her home address is given as number 3 Gloucester Lane, where the killing took place. Thomas Higgins, age 20 years died in hospital on the 28th December 1896 from Haemoptysis.

Anne was unfortunate in a sense, that like the victim, John McKenna, she too was in the wrong place at the wrong time. If she was indeed living at this address with her young family, she may have left her room to see what all the noise and shouting was about. According to the court and arrest records, the only thing Anne Higgins was really guilty off in relation to this murder was fetching and holding an oil lamp for Margaret Carroll, who was planning to rob the victim of all that he had on his person at the time of the assault. There is no evidence to suggest that Anne Higgins played an active role in the assault or manslaughter of John McKenna. Her sentence was certainly harsh for such a minor part in this drama and this must have played on her mind, as it did in a similar way, on the mind of fellow prisoner, C 956, John Byrne.

Courtroom sketch of Thomas P. Higgins, the son of Anne Higgins, one of the accused.

Anne Higgins petitioned the Lord Lieutenant many times, pleading for mercy and a reduction in the length of time she would have to spend in Mountjoy Prison. Somehow or other, it would appear that she had some knowledge that her end was near and was therefore anxious to once again set her eyes on her young family. Judging by the style of writing and the language used in these petitions it is obvious that a second party was involved in how they were presented. Each time she received the same reply, '*Let the law takes its course*. There was no mercy shown or given.

According to this entry on Anne Higgins prison record, shortly after her incarceration she wrote a letter to her son, Thomas whose address was 'Care of Mr Conlan, a publican from Gloucester Place, but seemingly received no reply. In 1897 Anne wrote to Rev. Ridgeway of the Pro Cathedral, this was most probably in relation to her children's situation. On the 20th February 1898, she wrote a letter to a Miss Julia Higgins. She may be the eldest of her three daughters.

Name and Residence of Family. (Husband, Wife, Parent, or next of kin, &c.) (Nature of relationship.)	Address at time of Apprehension	Education	Religion (Any subsequent change to be recorded here, with date).
Thos P. Higgins (son) c/o Mr Conlon (Publican) Gloucester Place, Dublin	3 Gloucester Lane, Dublin	R. W	Roman Catholic

Crime of which convicted, (as given in Rule of Court.) and place where it was committed.		Committal	Conviction	Sentence (years)
Manslaughter. (3 Gloucester Lane Dublin)	on Remand	6th July 96	5th Aug 1896.	Five (5)
	Date for trial	13th July 96		Post Sentence
	Place	Dublin	Green Street Courthouse	Police Supervision
	Court	D. M. Police Court	Co. of City of Dublin City Commission Commencing 4.896	20

If the Convict's Licence become forfeited or revoked, the particulars of the offence resulting in such forfeiture or revocation will be entered below, at the receiving prison.

© National Archives

Anne Higgins was convicted on the 5th August 1896.

Statement showing date of Reception, and Trade followed at each Prison.

Prison	Date			Trade or Occupation	Signature of Superintendent or Officer in Charge
	Day	Month	Year		
Grangegorman Local	13	7	96	sewing + knitting	P. J. McCarthy
Grangegorman Convict	13	8	96	sewing + knitting	P. J. McCarthy
Mountjoy (Fem) Convict	25	8	97	sewing + knitting	P. J. McCarthy

(This Document is not to be folded.)

© National Archives

Anne Higgins work schedule while in prison from 1896-1897 was similar to that of Nannie McLoughlin and Margaret Carroll, sewing and knitting. She too was granted points for each workshop she attended and was also allowed points for any time she spent in hospital or was considered unfit for work. A note from the hospital or prison doctor was attached to her prison file each time she was excused from work and granted points for her absence.

© National Archives

It would appear that Anne Higgins had very few visitors while in Grangegorman Women's Prison from 1896-1897. Her first visitor, on the 22nd August 1896 was Bridget Finn; she is the mother of two of the co-accused, Nannie McLoughlin and Margaret Carroll. Bridget also visited her two daughters in prison and possible brought news of each one with her as she did her rounds. This particular visit was made shortly after Anne was locked away. Being sent to prison for five years must have come as quite a shock to Anne Higgins. At 42 years of age she was no longer a young woman and on several previous occasions had only spent short periods of time locked up. She appears to have spent most of her prison time going in and out of hospital. In August of 1896 she is diagnosed as having Peritonitis, an inflammation of the Peritoneum, typically caused by bacterial infection, either through the blood or after the rupture of an abdominal organ. Time was running out for Anne Higgins.

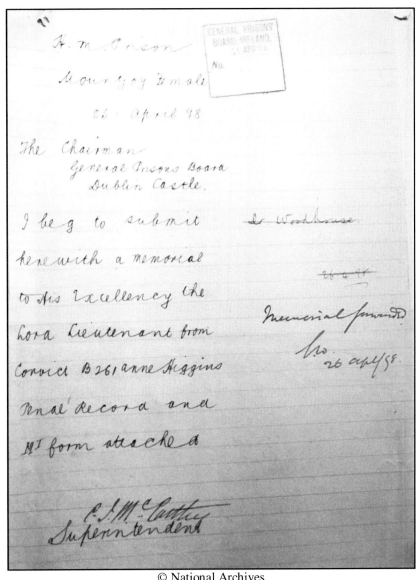

'I beg to submit herewith a memorial to his Excellency, from convict, B 261, Anne Higgins'.

April 1898, Petition from Anne Higgins to the Lord Lieutenant.

My Lord,

I most respectfully beg to state I was arrested on the 4th July 1896 on a charge of manslaughter and was sentenced to five years penal servitude. I am innocent of the crime I am charged with. I am in a very bad state of health and I am under the Doctor's care in hospital 16 months and no hope of getting better. I have six children outside without a father, three little girls and three boys. I had seven but one died since I came in here. He was our chief support and would have looked after the others.

I have not heard or seen anything about them since the 3rd May last. I am in a bad state of mind. I therefore most humbly implore your Excellency to be pleased to take my case into your kind consideration and for the sake of my poor children to be pleased to order my discharge in order that I may have the consolation of seeing them before I die and your petition, as is duty bound, will ever pray.

Anne Higgins.

'Pay up or get out…'

On the 3rd December 1899, eighteen months after submitting her petition, a reply was received from the Lord Lieutenant which basically states *"Let the law take its course"*. This reporting also states that Anne's health is indifferent; she was in hospital for nothing more serious than Piles and Debility (feeling weak). Doctor Woodhouse, the prison doctor said that her present illness was not of a serious nature and that he saw no reason, on the grounds of health, for recommending an early release. And yet, not too soon afterwards, the prison medical team were quite aware that Anne Higgins had only a relatively short time left to live.

The report also says that a judge wrote, that he could not recommend a reduction in any of the sentences related to this case. He said that he had a similar request from Annie's fellow prisoner, John Byrne. This news must have come as a great and saddened disappointment to Anne Higgins. Everyone in authority was aware that Anne Higgins was dying and they still insisted that the law must take its course.

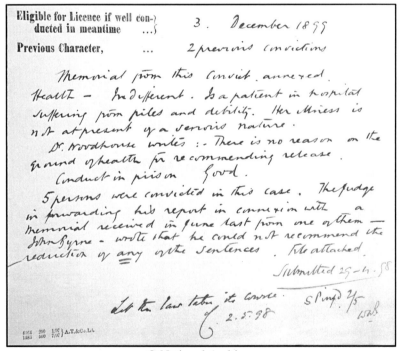

'Let the law take its course'

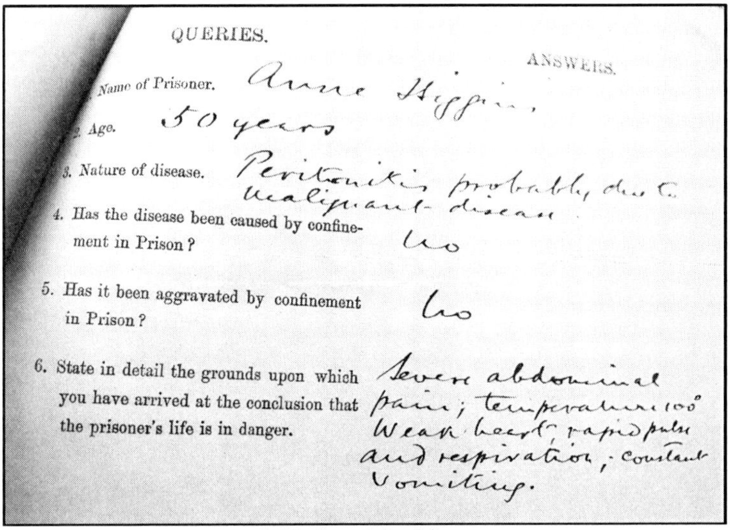

© National Archives

Anne Higgins was 42 years old when first arrested in 1896 and two years later, in 1898 she is 50 years old.

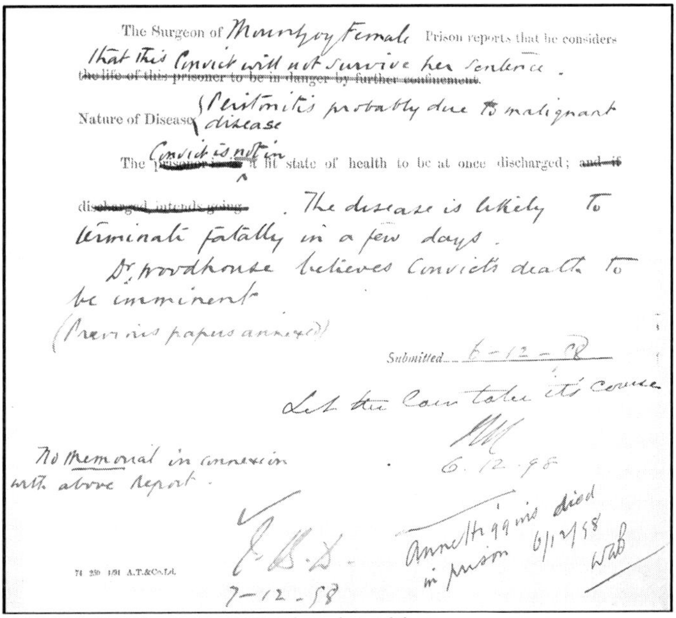

© National Archives

'This convict will not survive her sentence…'

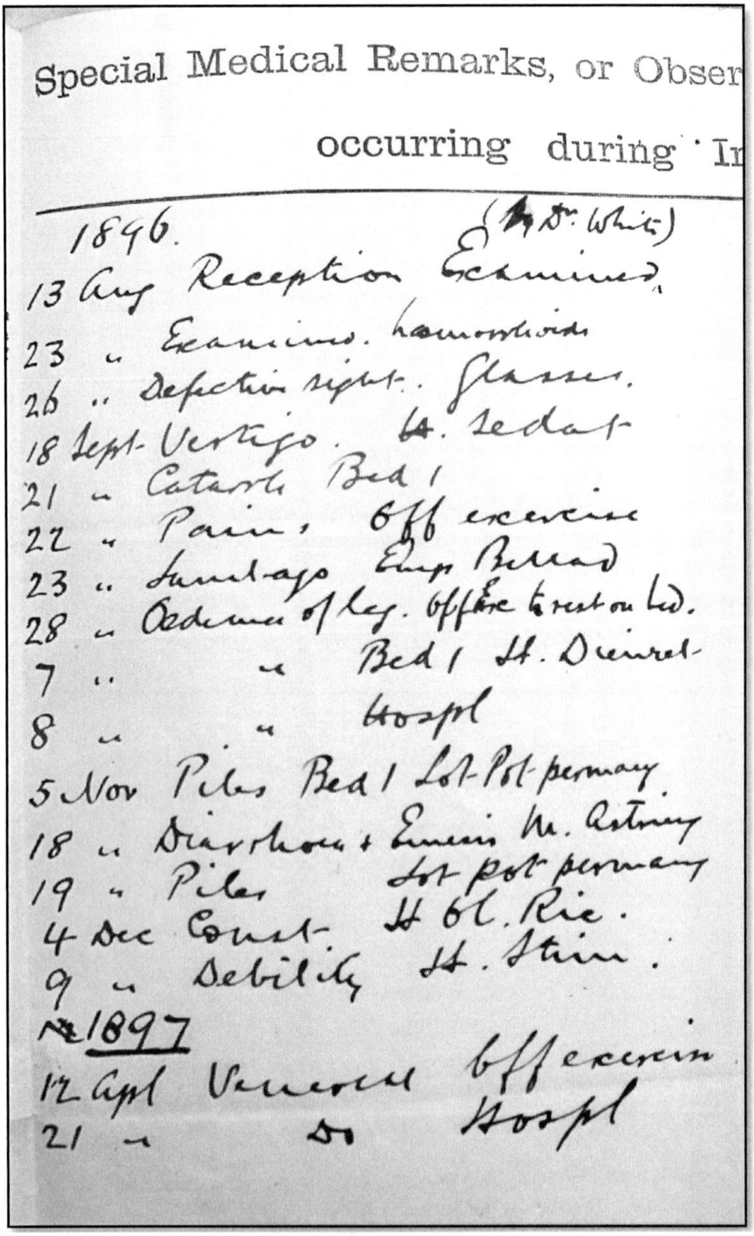

1896.   (~ Dr. White)

13 Aug Reception Examined,

23 "   Examined. haemorrhoids

26 "   Defective sight. glasses.

18 Sept. Vertigo.   bt. sedat

21 "   Catarrh Bed 1

22 "   Pain,   off exercise

23 "   Lumbago Emp Bellad

28 "   Oedema of leg. Offre to rest on bed.

7   "   "   Bed 1 St. Dieurel-

8   "   "   Hospl

5 Nov Piles Bed 1 Lot Pot permang.

18 "   Diarrhoea + Enuris M. Astrung

19 "   Piles   Lot pot permang

4 Dec Const-   H bt. Ric.

9   "   Debility   St. Stim .

№ 1897

12 Apl Venereal   off exercise

21 "   "   Hospl

© National Archives

According to this medical report of 1896/97 Anne Higgins
suffered from haemorrhoids, defective sight, vertigo, catarrh,
oedema of the legs (swelling), diarrhoea and Venereal Efficacy.

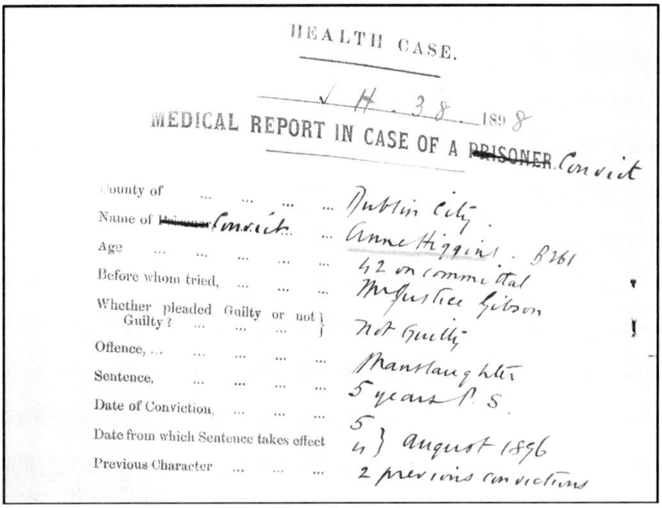

© National Archives

A not guilty plea.

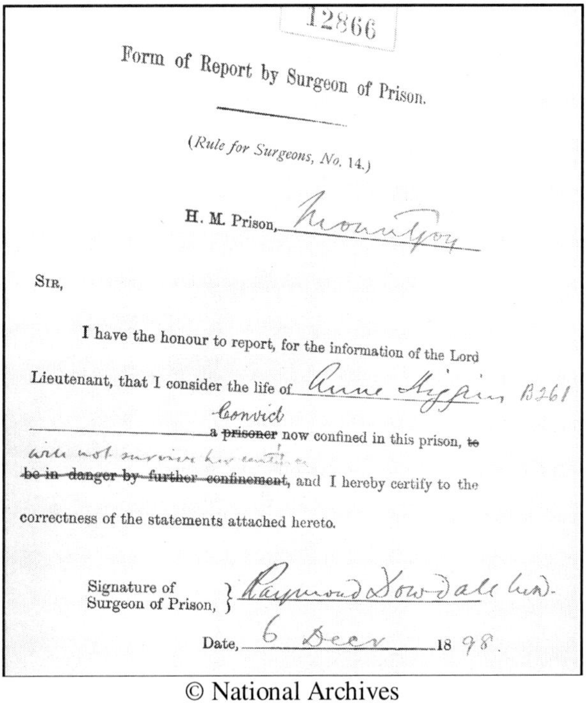

© National Archives

Prison Surgeon's concern for Anne Higgins in December 1898.

This report on Anne Higgins states that she was admitted to hospital for treatment. She was diagnosed with Acute Peritonitis. The doctor said that she was not fit to be removed and that her death was imminent.

MOUNTJOY CONVICT'S DEATH.

Yesterday a convict named Anne Higgins died in Mountjoy Prison, where she had been confined since August, '95, undergoing a sentence of five years' penal servitude for manslaughter. She had been under treatment in the prison hospital for fourteen months.

Evening Herald Newspaper Report 1898

© National Archives

Prisoner B 261, Anne Higgins died in prison.

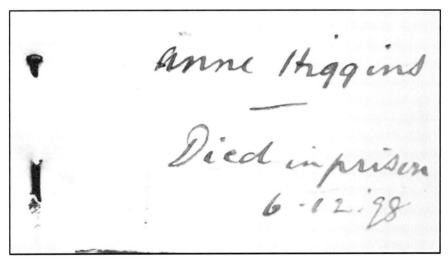

© National Archives

A note attached to Anne Higgins prison file. She was buried in a pauper's grave in Saint Patrick's section, WI 11 of Glasnevin Cemetery. Her age is given as 42 years old and she was a Labourers wife.

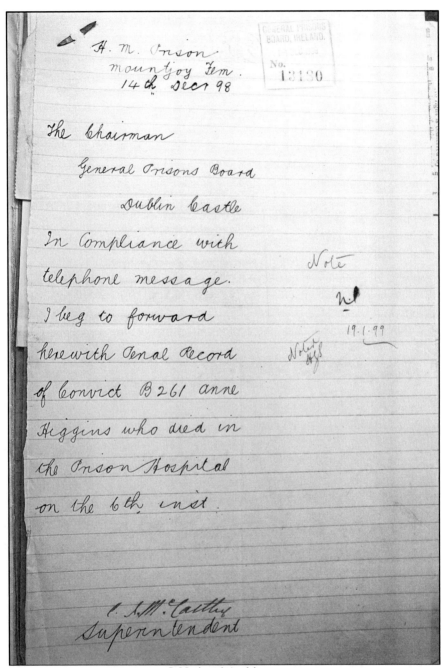

H. M. Prison
Mountjoy Fem.
14th Secr 98

The Chairman

General Prisons Board

Dublin Castle

In Compliance with

telephone message.

Note

w.

19.1.99

I beg to forward

herewith Penal Record

Note off

of Convict B 261 Anne

Higgins who died in

the Prison Hospital

on the 6th inst.

C. M. McCarthy
Superintendent

© National Archives

The final word on Anne Higgins.

Chapter 12

John Byrne

© National Archives

Convict C 956, John Byrne, Mountjoy Prison, 1896. The 3rd finger on his right hand is broken.

Rarely if ever has a more gruesome, sordid, and despairful case occupied the attention of an Irish jury than that which came to a termination yesterday in the Dublin Commission Court. The story told by the evidence reveals a horrible depth of infamy and callous criminality. There will be general agreement with two observations of the judge. In the course of the trial the judge declared, whatever the cost, the district where these shoals of vice and crime pursue their victims should not be left in darkness during the darkest hours of night in order to effect a small economy in the city gas bill. The gas was turned off just as the police sergeant who found the unfortunate victim of the crime was examining the body. This was at 1.20 a.m. The public will sympathise with the protest of his lordship. They will also sympathise with the doubts which he entertained as to the sufficiency of the sentences imposed. Let us hope they will be sufficient, nevertheless, to save the community from the perpetration of another such crime in its midst.

Copy of a newspaper report attached to the prison file of Convict, C 956, John Byrne in 1896.

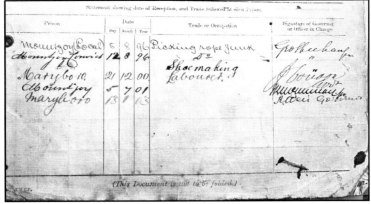

While serving a part of his sentence in Mountjoy Prison in 1896, John Byrne was assigned to pick Junk. This was the name given to old ropes and cables once used on ships. These were cut up and then finely picked into fibres to create oakum. Oakum was then mixed with tar or grease and used as caulking to fill in the gaps between the wooden planks of ships to make them watertight.

John Byrne's previous convictions.

A description of John Byrne in 1896. The 3rd finger on his right hand is broken and he has a short cocked nose.

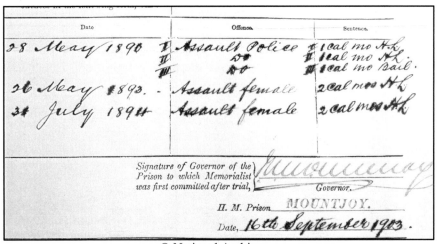

John Byrne's prison record from 1890 to 1894, prior to his arrest for murder in 1896. Three times he was imprisoned for assaulting members of the police force and twice for assaulting women.

In 1897 John Byrne applied for *'A Discharge of Convict'*. On this application it was noted that the police never knew John Byrne to live by honest means. A Supt. O'Reilly stated that the evidence presented by Higgins, that he played no part in the death of John McKenna was false. O'Reilly went on to say that *'Byrne carried the deceased man, after he received some injury in the house, 3 Gloucester Lane, from the door of said house and threw him in the lane. Higgins gave instructions to Nannie McLoughlin, Margaret Carroll and Anne Higgins to "Leave him there until I do for him". It was proven that Byrne then kicked the deceased as he lay in the lane and then rifled his pockets'*. This application also noted that John Byrne was convicted on three previous occasions. His request was denied. Supt. O'Reilly went on to say that *"Byrne was for many years and up to the time of his arrest, living with thieves and prostitutes and upon the proceeds of prostitution and robbery. It is not known that he ever lived by an honest occupation. I submit that if liberated it is most likely that he will join his former companions and associates in crime"*. In addition to the women above, John McLoughlin was also convicted of the same crime.

Thomas Lynam

Inspector

Dublin Metropolitan Police

Summerhill Station, C Division, 24th June 1897

Petition to the Lord Lieutenant from John Byrne

That petitioner was charged with the crime of murder committed in Gloucester Lane on the 4th July 1896 and of this charge petitioner is not guilty. Petitioner humbly pleads to your Excellency to review his case as the witness against petitioner committed gross perjury which if the depositions are examined it will be seen. She swore positively that she was in receipt of a weekly wage of ten shillings and was of irreproachable character before the magistrate. But admitted before the judge that she was of the unfortunate class and had been in prison for receiving stolen goods and then admitted that she got no wages at all. The petitioner made a voluntary true statement as given Crown Evidence before the magistrate. The judge asking for its production at the trial but the prosecutor declined to do so and had he complied a true verdict would have been returned against the female prisoner and petitioner acquitted, for she hid a poker under her apron. John McLoughlin, the husband of the female prisoner was prepared to swear to the full entire innocence of petitioner but his evidence would not be allowed. The jury unhesitatingly withdrew the capital charge and his Lordship, the judge passed sentence of ten years penal servitude on petitioner and seven years on the woman that did the deed. And yet the petitioner was sentenced to a large portion of his lifetime on the contradictory evidence of a woman of evil report, a testimony taken in ludicrous opposition to all the rules of evidence. Petitioner therefore humbly asks your Excellency to take a merciful view of his case and grant a remission of his sentence as the Crown supressed the statement which would have set petitioner free and petitioner, as duty bound, will ever pray.

C 956 John Byrne

28th June 1900

Petition to the Lord Lieutenant from John Byrne

That petitioner was charged with the crime of murder committed in Gloucester Lane on the 4th July 1896 and of this charge petitioner is not guilty. Petitioner made a voluntary true statement as given Crown Evidence and this statement was signed in the witness box by petitioner and counter signed by the magistrate. The judge asked for its production at the trial. The prosecutor declined to do so and had he complied a true verdict would have been returned against the female prisoner and petitioner acquitted. The jury unhesitatingly withdrew the capital charge and his Lordship, the judge passed sentence of ten years penal servitude on petitioner and seven years on the woman that did the deed. And yet the petitioner was sentenced to a large portion of his lifetime on the contradictory evidence of a woman of evil repute. Petitioner therefore humbly begs that his Excellence will use clemency as the crown.

John Byrne

12th April 1901

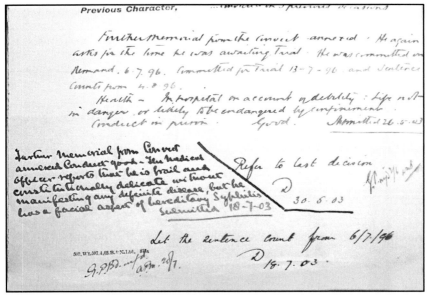

Congenital Syphilis

John Byrne had Congenital Syphilis, a condition that was acquired by the foetus from his mother during pregnancy and present at birth. This would sometimes manifest itself in the form of severe early skin rashes, often occurring in the first 10 weeks of life, bone and cartilage defects, liver and kidney disturbances, deafness, peg teeth, saddle-shaped nose, scars at the angles of the mouth and damage to the corneas in the form of Interstitial Keratitis. The cornea is the transparent front part of the eye that covers the iris, pupil, and anterior chamber. Interstitial Keratitis is a serious condition in which blood vessels grow into the cornea. Such growth can cause loss of the normal clearness of the cornea, resulting in red and watery eyes. This information was contained in a report from 1903 in reply to a plea submitted by John Byrne requesting that his sentence time should have begun on the day of his arrest while awaiting trial in 1896 and not on the day he was first imprisoned for his role in the manslaughter of John McKenna. His request was finally granted, which meant that he had one week less of his sentence to serve. In the National Archives, Dublin there is a prison file of petitions relating to John Byrne that show he had submitted at least one petition per month for several years in relation to this subject.

© National Archives

'Convict C 956, John Byrne, most respectfully begs to apply to his Excellency for the period he was awaiting trial during which period he was engaged at the usual prison labour and trusts that his conduct since admission to prison has earned for Petitioner the kind consideration of his humble request for which Petitioner will ever pray'.

Judges Report on the Case

Gloucester Lane Murder

Sir,

I have the honour to submit my report for the misfortunates and their Excellency's. The prisoner, with John McLoughlin, T.P Higgins and three women was indicted before me in 1896 for the wilful murder of John McKenna. The deceased man, who was of powerful physique, married with a family, in permanent employment with the Railway, on the 3rd July met a girl, a prostitute named Thompson who took him to her room in Gloucester Lane. The rooms were let by Mrs McLoughlin, one of the prisoners and wife of John McLoughlin. The man paid Margaret Carroll, another of the prisoners for the room. The girl and he lay down when nannie McLoughlin came in and after asking for whiskey gave the girl a terrible blow on the head with an empty bottle. He ran downstairs covered with blood. The people in the house followed and she heard a sound of beating below followed by moans. A neighbour, Catherine Dillon of number 2 Gloucester Lane, another brothel, heard the woman's screams and looking out, thought she saw Thompson running away. She heard Byrne, the prisoner, say "I am not done with him yet", Nannie McLoughlin asked for the poker. They then dragged unfortunate McKenna out. Byrne and McLoughlin kicked him lying on the ground. Maggie Carroll searched his pockets and took what was there. She said to Byrne there was gold. They then dragged him away down the lane. The five then went to a Shebeen for porter. The body with the pockets turned inside out was found by police at about 1.30am. The man was snoring heavily; he died soon after in consequence. The cause of death was a fracture at the base of the skull and laceration to the brain. The fracture might have been caused by a blow or a severe fall. The prisoners, when arrested made statements. The man's silver watch was pawned by John McLoughlin, other small articles were found on the premises.

My opinion on the case was that the man, who had money and a watch, was attacked immediately (by) the girl, Thompson and either struck with a hammer or flung down the stairs on his head and then dragged out and robbed. The crime seemed to me very like murder and was, I thought, in fact murder. The male bully's, like brothers, living with and on the women, who were prostitutes, belong to a most dangerous class. Byrne, on his arrest, was much under the influence but afterwards made a willing statement of the event, putting the names on the others. He was a comparative young man but I thought his participation in the crime was influenced by the inducee.

I cannot recommend the reduction of any of the sentences, which were 10 years for each of the men and 7 and 5 years for the women.

John George Gibson

(No date given)

Schoolmaster's report on John Byrne in 1901.

By all accounts, it seems that John Byrne behaved himself in prison. The fact that he could read and write helped him in being promoted from one level of learning to another. By the time he was released in 1903 he was quite capable of reading up to 5th Standard. In all of his time in prison, Byrne only ever received one letter, from his brother Patrick who also paid him a visit in Mountjoy Jail on two occasions. His aunt, Mrs Bridget Byrne from number 6 Dunne Street, Dublin also paid him a couple of visits in 1897 and 1901.

John Byrne was very angry at the injustice he felt was meted out to him, he felt that he had played a minor role in the death of John

McKenna, in comparison to that which was handed down to Nannie McLoughlin, whom he states was the person who committed the actual murder. In all of the hundreds of petitions that he submitted to the Lord Lieutenant, everyone contains this argument. He felt that he was in some way *"Set-Up"* by Nannie McLoughlin and even her own husband, John was willing to testify to that fact.

In his final days of imprisonment John Byrne's health began to fail. He was almost continually in hospital in his last year of imprisonment, suffering from debility. The doctor in Maryborough Prison described Byrne as a *"Puny Man"* and showing symptoms of Hereditary Syphilis.

© National Archives

Profile photo of John Byrne in 1903.

Subject:- Release on licence

H. M. Prison Maryboro'
4th December '03

Submitted
        The penal record
of convict C936 John Byrne
as he will have the required
number of marks. 21906
earned to qualify for
release on licence on 5th I Gov
prox, if his conduct   A + B approved
continues satisfactory in
the meantime   II Office
        He is taking his discharge
for Dublin, and his gratuity   Prepare licence
will be paid him through   for 29th inst.
the Prisoners Aid Society.
        This convict is in the Special   [initials]
Class and is eligible under
Rule 19 para -d, to be   5. 12. 03
recommended for an extra
remission not exceeding one | II Dow [initials] 5/12
week, which if approved, | A
would have him eligible |
for release on 29th inst.
        There are three previous
convictions of assault recorded
against this convict, and as he
was an associate of women
of the unfortunate class prior
to present offence, I recommend | B
that the obligation of reporting to |
police when released should be |
enforced
                        [signature]
The Chairman   Governor
General Prisons Board

© National Archives

Conditions of early release in 1903.

184

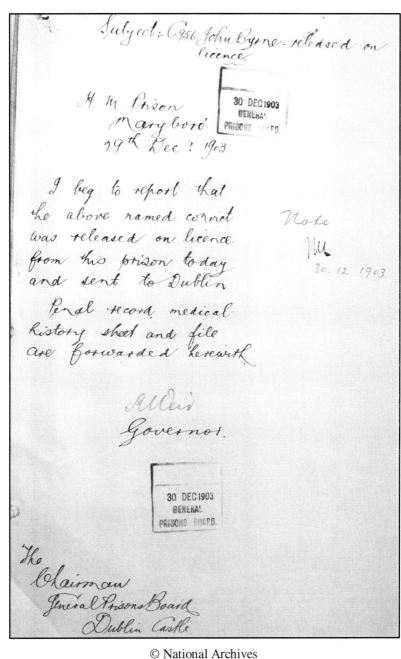

© National Archives

John Byrne released on license on the 30th December 1903 from Maryboro Prison, Portlaoise.

*Final prison photo of Convict C 956, John Byrne on his release
from Maryborough Prison in 1903.*

Chapter 13

Joe Finn

In 1917 Annie Carroll, daughter of Margaret Carroll eventually met up with her older brother, Joe Finn and his wife, Esther White. Annie had not seen Joe since they were separated in 1896. Joe had led a hard life since leaving the Christian Brothers in Artane Industrial School. In his late teenage years he was arrested for being drunk and disorderly. He then became involved in the running of a Shebeen. Joe had married Esther White in the Pro Cathedral, Dublin, in 1908. At this stage of his life Joe Finn was on a slippery and downward path of drink, violence and law breaking. At the time of his marriage he was living in 35 Upper Tyrone Street, present day Marlborough Street.

According to the 1911 Irish Census for Dublin, Joe and Esther Finn were sharing a house with Christopher Timmins, it was a small cottage type dwelling situated at the rere of 27 Mabbott Street (James Joyce Street/Corporation Street). There were three cottages in this lane but only one was occupied in 1911. There were two rooms in the cottage, one of which was occupied by Joe and Esther Finn. According to the census record, Joe and Esther had three children who had all died young. They did however, have more children at a later stage in their marriage.

Joe Finn was constantly in trouble with the law; he was arrested on several occasions for being drunk and abusive or being in some way involved in one Shebeen or another.

At one time Joe was employed as a Sack Maker. His marriage to Esther was fraught with difficulties because Joe was drunk and abusive to her on an almost daily basis and they both had served time in prison. Esther was almost a mirror image of the man she married, with her fondness for drink and fighting. On the 3rd of June 1924, 37 year old Joe Finn was admitted to the Mental Department of the South Dublin Union Hospital.

Derelict tenement houses overlooking Waterford Street.

In later years Joe told his sister, Annie Carroll that his wife, Esther had signed him in *'Under the Red Ink'* which basically meant that only she could sign him out. There is however, no evidence to back up Joe's claim. According to the hospital records, Joe Finn was married with three children. He lived in 22 Marlborough Place, Dublin. It seems from the information contained on the hospital records that Joe had suffered some kind of attack that lasted two days, as a result of which, he was declared insane. This is most probably why Esther signed him into the Union or he could have been taken in by the police.

Esther White was married to Joe Finn.

Joe Finn spent at least eight years in Artane Industrial School.

This report also stated that Joe was destitute and had no friends who were willing or able to support him.

On the 1st of December 1925, Joe Finn was transferred to Grangegorman Lunatic Asylum. The Union report stated that Joe Finn was deemed to be very violent and a danger not only to himself but also to those around him. He kept telling the doctors that *'The hangman is waiting for my body'*. He also stated that he wanted to kill somebody and smashed a window by throwing his shoe at it. He was also constantly assaulting other patients. It is because of this kind of behaviour that Joe found himself being transferred to the Grangegorman Lunatic Asylum. A Peace Commissioner from Westland Row signed a form stating that Joe Finn was *'of unsound mind and a proper person to be taken charge of and detained as a patient in Grangegorman Mental Hospital'*.

Joe's sister, Annie Carroll and her friend, Mary Vincent regularly visited him on an almost weekly basis, they also brought along Annie's five year old daughter, Mary Carroll.

The gateway into Grangegorman Lunatic Asylum.

According to his death certificate, Joe Finn died on Saturday the 30th of October 1926, from Tuberculosis, a bacterial infection spread through inhaling tiny droplets from the coughs or sneezes of an infected person. Joe Finn's sister, Annie Carroll later said that when she and Mary Vincent viewed his body in the Asylum Morgue, Joe's head was wrapped in bandages and that his upper body was covered in bruises. She came to the conclusion that Joe must have been in a fight or was given a beating the night before his death. Another of the inmates, who had slept in the same Ward as Joe Finn, later told Annie that a staff member was trying to steal Joe's money from under his pillow and they got into a fight over it.

(2)

26772

Richmond District Asylum.

Ward No. _5._

Patient's Name _Joseph Finn_

Register No. _33602._

Died at _8.55_ o'clock, _P.m._, on _30th_ day of _October_ 1926

Removed to Mortuary _8 o'c a.m. 31st_ " "

When Interred or Removed _8.30 o'c P.m. 1st Nov._ "

By Whom _Esther Finn (wife) 22 Marlboro Place._

Nurse or Attendant present at Death _Peter Clerkin_

Dated _2/11/'26._

Michl Kenna.
Attendant.

N.B.—Christian Names to be written in full.

Joe Finn died on Saturday, the 30th October 1926; he was taken to the hospital morgue on Sunday the 31st October and removed for burial on Monday 1st November.

He said that Joe was eventually overpowered by three other members of staff and taken away. Joe Finn's body was claimed from the Asylum by his wife, Esther and he was buried in Glasnevin Cemetery. On the 25th of March 1930, Esther Finn remarried to William Butler. Esther died on the 2nd of December 1960 and she too is buried in Glasnevin Cemetery, Dublin.

Joe led such a different lifestyle to that of his sister, Annie Carroll. Would it have been any different if his mother had not been involved in the murder of John McKenna or prostitution? What chances in life did Joe Finn ever have that would see him rise to better circumstances than to that in which he was born? He was the illigimate son of an alcoholic prostitute, he never knew his father and at a very early stage in his life he found himself living under the harsh regime of the Irish Christian Brothers, where sexual, physical and mental abuse was rife. Shortly after his release from the Industrial School Joe stepped back into the sordid world in which his mother and her sisters lived. By the time he was twenty years of age, he was already a confirmed alcoholic with a criminal record and his marriage was a disaster. Are these perhaps, some of the demons that haunted the mind of Joe Finn, causing his mental instability, resulting in him being detained in Grangegorman Lunatic Asylum, where he eventually died?

Grangegorman Female Prison, where Margaret Finn was first incarcerated at 13 years of age, was situated directly across the road from the entrance gates to the Lunatic Asylum where her son, Joe Finn died in 1926.

Coat of Arms displayed above the original entrance to the North Dublin Union Workhouse, where Joe Finn was born.

Grangegorman Mental Hospital
VISITING PASS

Pass fr

5

24 March 1915

To...

....

On presenting this Order on SUNDAYS and WEDNESDAYS
between the hours of 11 a.m. and 12.30 p.m. you will be

allowed to visit your ....

the patient ....

Chief Resident Medical Superintendent.

NOTE.—Visiting passes cannot be granted for special hours
or days.

Visits are not permitted of children under 16 years of age.

WARNING.—Visitors are warned against bringing (a)
intoxicating drink, (b) medicines or drugs, (c) matches, or
(d) dangerous articles (such as knives, razors, or tools) to
patients. Letters from patients must not be taken out for
post or delivery. Any breach of these rules will result in the
withdrawal of Visiting Pass.

Visitors Pass for Grangegorman Mental Hospital.

In 1909, 29 year old Joe Finn is arrested for running a Shebeen with his wife, Esther.

19 year old Joe Finn arrested for being drunk and disorderly.

195

Chapter 14

Annie Carroll

Annie Carroll.

In 1917, Annie Carroll, the daughter of Margaret Carroll, who had spent more than ten years under the care of the Presentation Sisters in Cashel Reform School, County Tipperary was now returning to Dublin with her three year old son, John. Since leaving the Convent at 16 years of age, Annie had worked as a Domestic Servant for a Mrs Ryan of Bansha, County Tipperary. She then went to work for the Maher family; they had a farm, a pub and a shop, situated in a small townsland about two miles outside of Tipperary town. This family were very probably related to Jack Meagher who had a pub on the corner of Corporation Street and Purdon Street in Dublin and was also from Tipperary. Annie had become very attached to the Maher family and must have found it very distressing when she was leaving them in Tipperary for her journey to Dublin.

Throughout her adult life in Tipperary Annie Carroll may have kept up a correspondence with her mother in Dublin and it may have been through these letters that she learned of her mother being seriously ill and near death. Had Annie an understanding of her mother's past, did she ever learn of the murder of John McKenna? If so, she never shared this information with any of her children.

Annie had also led a different lifestyle to her brother, Joe Finn and this may be thanks in part to the Industrial School where she spent her younger days under the care of the Presentation Sisters, who gave her a relatively good education and a very different perspective on life than that of the one Joe Finn had. One story in particular that Annie's daughter, Mary tells about her mother's time in Cashel is as follows, '***She said she always had long hair and she was looking over the bannisters in the orphanage and some girl caught her hair and then let it go. My mother lost her balance and went over and went down onto the marble floor and damaged her eye. It was never looked after properly and then when she came home here, the time of the Black and Tans, she had to go up to the Eye and Ear Hospital and she'd be trying to dodge them. Her eye was never looked after properly. She still had her eye but she could never see anything, but still she could see you a mile away***'.

Maggie Gorman, a decent woman from Railway Street.

The Dublin Annie Carroll came back to was very different to the one she had left at five years of age. This was certainly not the Dublin Annie imagined it to be. Many buildings in the main thoroughfare of Sackville Street (O'Connell Street) were still in ruins as a result of the 1916 uprising. The General Post Office too was only a shadow of its former glory. Most of the remaining buildings and shops in and around the G.P.O. were almost completely destroyed.

The large crowds of people that Annie encountered as she walked through the busy streets of Dublin must have seemed to her almost bigger than the population of Tipperary town. There were still armed police and soldiers patrolling the streets and prostitution was

Mary Carroll, daughter of Annie Carroll and grand-daughter of Margaret Carroll nee Finn.

still rife in the area where her mother lived. The Dublin accents and twangs must also have seemed very strange to her ears compared to the Tipperary accent she was so used to. The smells and sounds of Dublin were now so alien to her and her young son, sounds and smells that were once a part of her younger life in the city of her birth. Annie also discovered that her father, Patrick Carroll had died some years previous, as had her younger brother, Christopher Patrick. Annie also discovered that her mother was now remarried, to Christopher McDonnell.

Surname	Forename	Townland/Street	DED	County	Age	Sex
McMahon	Marianne	St. Francis Abbey - Friar St.	Cashel Urban	Tipperary	10	F
Todd	Lizzie	St. Francis Abbey - Friar St.	Cashel Urban	Tipperary	12	F
Grant	Marianne	St. Francis Abbey - Friar St.	Cashel Urban	Tipperary	12	F
Mc Evoy	Mary	St. Francis Abbey - Friar St.	Cashel Urban	Tipperary	9	F
Kinahan	Catherine	St. Francis Abbey - Friar St.	Cashel Urban	Tipperary	13	F
Kinahan	Alice	St. Francis Abbey - Friar St.	Cashel Urban	Tipperary	11	F
Carroll	Annie	St. Francis Abbey - Friar St.	Cashel Urban	Tipperary	10	F
Moore	Margaret	St. Francis Abbey - Friar St.	Cashel Urban	Tipperary	15	F
Fogarty	Ellen	St. Francis Abbey - Friar St.	Cashel Urban	Tipperary	14	F
Ward	Bridget	St. Francis Abbey - Friar St.	Cashel Urban	Tipperary	11	F

Annie Carroll on the 1901 census for the Presentation Sisters in Cashel Reform School, County Tipperary.

How must Annie Carroll have felt walking into a run-down area of Dublin where her mother lived, with its tall dirty tenement houses and filthy side streets? How different did the scruffy young children of this area appear to her in comparison to the children of the orphanage in Tipperary where everything and everyone was washed and scrubbed clean on a daily basis? Did she ever keep in touch with the Maher family that she had left behind? For several years after her return to Dublin, Annie bought the Tipperary newspaper every week, so she obviously liked to keep up to date with news from that area.

On the 2nd of February 1915, Margaret Carroll was married to Christopher McDonnell in Dublin's Pro Cathedral. She was living back in the Monto at this stage and renting a room in 20 Railway Street. Sometime in 1912, Margaret's son, Joe Finn was finally released from Artane Industrial School and may have lived with his mother at this address. It was here also that Margaret met and was befriended by a young prostitute by the name of Mary Vincent.

***John Darcy and his wife, Bridget Brown with a 'Monto Baby'
they found and reared as their own.***

Mary Vincent was born about 1886/87. She was an abandoned
baby that came into the care of the Workhouse Authorities, who
arranged for her to be fostered out as a *'Nursing Child'*. In 1901,
life for Mary Vincent appeared to be as near perfect when at 16
years of age she was legally adopted by her Foster Parents. She was
living in a relatively good family environment in Templeogue,
County Dublin and was not considered illiterate as she could read
and write, unlike many other children and adults of that time.

However, on the 7th November 1906, 20 year old, servant girl, Mary Vincent was arrested for being in Portobello Army Barracks. She was taken to Rathmines Police Station where it was noted that Mary was a prostitute, she was later discharged. Whatever happened to Mary that she chose this path in life? It was also said of Mary Vincent that she was a great friend to Countess Markievics of 1916 fame and had once studied to be a Teacher, finding work in a school in Terenure, County Dublin. Mary would also remain a great friend to Margaret Carrol/McDonnell and later to her daughter, Annie Carroll. Not too unlike Margaret, Mary Vincent had spent most of her young life in and out of prison cells and was very much involved in the world of prostitution throughout those years. Mary Vincent was last arrested for prostitution in 1917.

© National Archives

In 1899, Margaret Carroll wrote to the Reform School in Cashel, County Tipperary inquiring about her daughter, Annie Carroll.

After the death of her mother in 1917, Annie Carroll took on the job of cleaning and polishing offices belonging to Solicitors in nearby Mountjoy Square. While she was living in number 11 Elliott Place, nearby Publican, Joe O'Rielly offered Annie a job looking after his invalid wife at their house in the Dublin suburb of Drumcondra. In return for this Joe allowed Annie and her family to move into the flat above his pub. In later years when the pub was being demolished Annie was offered a new flat, recently built by Dublin Corporation, in Avondale House, Cumberland Street. Annie died in 1964 in Colchester, Essex, England, while on her first ever holiday away from home.

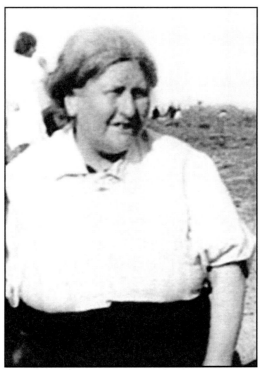

Monto prostitute, Mary Vincent.

'So she told you the same thing, did she'?

On the Run.

Chapter 15

'What's Your Name Again'?

Name changing had played a major role in the lives of most prostitutes from the Monto and especially those of Nannie McLoughlin, Bridget Nutter and my great-grandmother, Margaret Carroll, the three sisters involved in the telling of this story. One might assume, at this point in the story that the role of name-changing in the family ends here and that with the eventual destruction of the Monto, this way of life would also disappear. Let me take this story one step further, if only to prove a point.

On the 5th July 1919 my mother was born in the Rotunda Hospital, Dublin, where she was registered as Mary Carroll. This was the name chosen by her mother, Annie Carroll daughter of Margaret Carroll *'Prisoner B260'*. Annie's friend, Mary Spellman nee Vincent, former prostitute, came to visit Annie in the maternity hospital and ended up taking the new-born baby home with her while Annie was recovering from the birth. For some strange reason Mary Spellman would often tell people that the baby was her child. It was sometimes said that she had lost a baby of her own in the same hospital.

A few days after leaving the maternity ward, Mary Spellman and a group of her like-minded friends brought baby Mary Carroll to Our Lady of Lourdes Church in Sean McDermot Street to be christened. However, every time Mary Spellman and her friends came to a pub on their way to the church, they had to go in for a

Georgian Ironwork and a Tenement Doorway in Dublin.

drink to celebrate and whet the baby's head. So by the time they reached the church for the baptism, they were all well and truly inebriated and merry. When asked by the priest what name the baby was to be known by, Mary Spellman answered *'Mary Agnes Spellman'*, this of course, was her own name and not the name that Annie Carroll had chosen for her new baby. Is it possible then, that Mary Spellman made a mistake, thinking that the priest had asked what her own name was, and thereby ensuring that the child ended up with the wrong name?? So from then on this baby ended up being known on all Church Records as Mary Agnes Spellman and not Mary Carroll.

When Mary Carroll was a young girl, her mother, Annie Carroll married John Burke and Mary became known on her school records as Mary Burke. In 1938 when my mother married my father, Bernard Coffey in the Pro Cathedral, she was asked to produce a copy of her baptism certificate and not her birth certificate. She was then married under the name of Spellman and so, once again changing her name, she became Mary Agnes Coffey. Throughout the rest of her life everyone knew her as Aggie but her true name is Mary.

In later years I decided to apply for a Passport. When I went to the relevant office I asked for assistance in filling out my application form. It was at this point that the assistant looked at me and said *'And what is your mother's maiden name'*? I thought about this for a moment or two and said *'Take your pick'*. I had never been asked that question before and was unsure as to what name to give. The assistant used her computer to troll through official birth records looking for my name associated with Mary Carroll but to no avail. After several more tries she finally came up with Mary Agnes Spellman as my mother. So on my birth certificate and those of my 14 siblings, our mother's maiden name is written down as Spellman. I later asked my mother about this and she told me that she thought her mother may have been married three times. Another time I asked my father about this and he said *'Don't ask me, I don't know who I married'*. Another mystery that came to light is found on my mother's birth certificate. It states that her father is James Carroll and her mother's maiden name is Finn. In actual fact, my mother

207

In 1916, Monto Madam, Maggie Doyle had a steel door put up on the entrance into her Shebeen in Elliott Place. By the time the Police would eventually get the door open all of her customers and her illegal booze were safely out of the way

Two 'Old Timers' in the Monto.

never knew who her actual birth father was and her mother, Annie Carroll's maiden name is not Finn. Annie's father however, is Patrick Carroll and her mother is Margaret Finn. So who is James Carroll and why Finn?

Without having a clear knowledge of the history of my mother's various Christian names, I decided to delve a little deeper into this side of my family's history to see if I could uncover anything that would help me to understand the mind-set of a generation of people from times past that adopted this way of name changing. Was my mother's story a once off piece of flawed thinking or was it a cultural dilemma? I had no idea where this thought process was about to lead me.

What I did know from my mother was that she never had a problem with her Christian name being changed nor did any of the people from the neighbourhood where she grew up as a child, it was the norm. In fact, she said that she had a very happy childhood growing up in the heart of Dublin's Monto district, regardless of which name she was known by.

Julia Farrell

Julia Farrell, standing in Purdon Street near to the corner of Elliott Place. When her sister became widowed she left her three young children with the Nuns in the Magdalene Convent until she could better her situation. She was eventually handed back two children, the Nuns told her that she had only left two children with them. She later had a breakdown and ended her days in Grangegorman Lunatic Asylum.

Elliott Place.

The houses in Elliott Place had four rooms in each house and a family in each room. It was not unusual to find prostitutes sleeping on the bare floors at the top of the stairs in these houses. Some of the rooms were no longer than the length of a single bed and no wider than four feet. The downstairs windows of number ten, where the young boy stands, were blocked up by the father of this family in order to prevent his young children from seeing the activities of the Prostitutes outside on the corner. Margaret Carroll lived upstairs in number 11. The young boy standing by the window is Denis Doyle, his grandmother; Maggie Doyle was a 'Monto Madam' who sometimes rented out rooms in number 10 and other houses, to Prostitutes. She lived in number 14 Elliott Place, which she often turned into a Shebeen. When she was once arrested for this the Judge threw her case out when he realised who she was, He was one of her more regular customers.

Monto friends (including Paddy Coffey wearing his cap). The four young children are all 'Monto Babies', abandoned by their mother's and adopted into the Monto way of life.

Johnnie Marney, Blacker Doyle, Bessie McKeever, Murrier Meehan, Mousie Meehan, Barney Doyle and Jack McKeever 1930's.

Young children very often played and roamed amongst the fallen rubble of torn down tenement houses. In 1913 two dishevelled tenement houses collapsed in Church Street, Dublin killing seven people, including three young children.

Willie Gorman and Mary Anne (Gracie) Doyle.

Epilogue

There is very little remaining, if anything of the original Monto as it is described in this book. There are no tall tenement houses to be seen, no dark lanes or alleyways with seedy looking terraced houses and noisy Shebeens. Most of the original streets and lanes are gone too. The general layout of Railway Street, Foley Street, Beaver Street and Corporation Street however, are still the same but look nothing like they did originally. Along with the Prostitutes, Pimps and Madams of old, they have all faded into a misty past of song and story. However, there is one lane in particular that has never changed its name and little of its shape, Gloucester Lane, where John McKenna was killed. It is still there to be seen today, almost in its original form.

By 1896 the Monto was on its last legs with many of the tenement houses in wreck and ruin. It was no longer a fashionable place to be seen in and sexually transmitted diseases amongst prostitutes were rampant. Dublin was no longer viewed by many outsiders as the '*Jewel in the Crown*' of the British Empire.

In the early 1900's the Monto had become a hive for all sorts of illegal activities and political manoeuvres. In the later years of 1923-1925 and with the withdrawal of British troops out of Ireland, a religious mission led by Frank Duff with his Legion of Mary and Father Devane, and with the support of the General Police Commission, set about the successful closure of all of the brothels in this area of Dublin.

After the murder trial, Nannie McLoughlin and Margaret Carroll also faded into memory. Nanny had emigrated to New York, leaving her past behind and starting her life anew. Margaret however, lived on for a few more years in the Monto. With her youthful looks all but gone and her reputation too well known because of her role in the murder of John McKenna, Margaret Carroll eventually died in 1917. She left behind her son, Joe and her daughter, Annie, both of whom went on to have children of their own and whose families are still living today. Nothing further is known of John McKenna's widow and their children. In 1911 they were no longer living in Henrietta Street.

Perhaps this book should have been titled *'Half-Truths, Lies and Cover-Ups'*, because that is mainly what those involved in this murder case practised, and in some ways perfected, for most of their lives. It was part of their everyday culture. Strangely enough, this murder story had never filtered down through Margaret Carroll's family; nobody was ever aware of her involvement in a murder or of her time spent in prison.

The truth of Margaret's past was never known to her present day family either, until recent times. For all of those years her skeletons were safely locked away. It only came to light when the author discovered a newspaper report on the court proceedings of the murder of John McKenna in 1896 and the likelihood of his great-grandmother being involved. It was then that the skeletons stepped gently out of their closet. Was Margaret's daughter, Annie ever aware of her mother's past activities and the role she played in the

'Try that for size'

death of John McKenna? If so, she never let it be known to any of her own children.

The saving grace for my grandmother, Annie Carroll was the fact that, as a very young child, she ended up in the care of the Presentation Sisters in Cashel, County Tipperary where the nuns instilled into her a totally different set of principals from that of her family background. On her return from Tipperary to the Monto in Dublin in 1917, she somehow managed to keep these two aspects of her life separate and individual, using her Tipperary principles to overcome any temptation to slip into the murky underworld of that in which her mother and brother had become a part of. Throughout her adult life she remained a very private woman who chose her friends carefully.

Throughout their lives, my parents and their siblings never once criticised the lifestyle or choices of their parents or the people from their old neighbourhood. They both went to school and played with young children whose mothers were prostitutes, all victims of different times and a different world than that in which we live today. They both believed that how you lived was more important than where you lived.

A list of Monto Prostitutes

1900-1924

Recorded from the Dublin Metropolitan Police Arrest Books.

"And how did Constable PC31 come to give you his helmet'?

The following lists are a selection of names, in alphabetical order and by date, of women from three streets, Purdon Street, Elliott Place and Faithful Place, situated in the heart of the Monto, who are named as Prostitutes on the Mountjoy Gaol General Register of Prisoners and on the Arrest Books of the Dublin Metropolitan Police, from 1900-1924. The majority of these prostitutes gave Elliott Place as their address. In many cases this was the address of their Madam.

The people from this area of Dublin never referred to these women as Prostitutes, they were always known as *'The Girls'*. The average age of a Prostitute in this area of Dublin in the early 1900's was 18 years. Some of these women were known to the authorities by more than one name and in some cases there are those who even had as many as 25 different names. In most cases the court record states the name, age, height, hair and eye colour, scars, tattoos, address, place of birth, next of kin or spouse, what the individual is charged with and their sentence or fine. The majority of offences are drink related or connected with some form of robbery, usually that of one of their clients.

A small percentage of these prostitutes attempted suicide and were either imprisoned or fined for it. The average height of these women is five feet tall. Each name on this list is a story in itself. This is only a selection of what is found on official records in this period of Dublin's history and not a complete list. Very few of these women show up on the 1901 or 1911 census.

Purdon Street, celebrating the 100th anniversary of Catholic Emancipation in 1923.

A

1905: **Lily Anderson**, 22 yrs, Prostitute from 51 Purdon Street. Lily was born in Liverpool, England.

1906: **Nellie Avington**, 42 yrs, Prostitute from 16 Elliott Place. Nellie was born in Manchester, England. Her son, Albert lived in number 6 Byrne's Square in the Monto.

B

1901, **Catherine Byrne**, 24 yrs, Prostitute from 8 Elliott Place. Born in Little Bray, County Wicklow.

1902: **Christina Browne**, 24 yrs, Prostitute from 4 Elliott Place. Her mother is Mrs Browne from County Galway.

1903: **Mary Brennan/Kelly**, 33 yrs, Prostitute from Purdon Street. Born in Purdon Street and has a deformed left hand.

1904, **Polly Ballard**, 30 yrs, Prostitute from Purdon Street.

1905: **Margaret Ballard**, 30 yrs, Prostitute from 2 Elliott Place. Her sister, Catherine Kelly lived in 111 Gardiner Street.

1906: **Julia Broe**, 23 yrs, Prostitute from 3 Elliott Place. Arrested for larceny in a brothel but later discharged. She was born in Inchicore, Dublin.

1907: **Julia Brown/Mallon**, 22 yrs, Prostitute from 3 Elliott Place. She was born in Baltinglass, County Wicklow.

1907: **Polly Boland**, 45 yrs, Prostitute from 13 Elliott Place. She was charged with larceny in a brothel.

1901: **Lizzie Barrett**, 34 yrs, Prostitute from Purdon Street. Born in Great Western Square, Phibsborough, Dublin.

1901: **Alice Barter**, 21 yrs, Prostitute from Elliott Place.

© Martin Coffey

A young 'Monto Baby' who was originally found abandoned by the side of the road.

1911: **Maggie/Alice Beatty**, 25 yrs, Prostitute from Elliott Place. Her father is Robert Barter from 12 Mabbott Street, Dublin.

1911: **Nora Byrne**, 21 yrs, Prostitute from 16 Elliott Place.

1912: **Christina Brown**, 29 yrs, Prostitute from 15 Elliott Place.

1912: **Mary Boylan**, 25 yrs, Prostitute from 3 Elliott Place. She was charged with larceny of a watch, sentenced to prison.

1913: **Margaret Butler**, 29 yrs, Prostitute form 15 Elliott Place. She was born in Baltiboy, County Wicklow. Her father is James Butler.

1913: **Bridget Black/Kathleen Dawson/Mary Whelan/Kate Black**, 19yrs, Prostitute from 10 Elliott Place. She was born in Waterford and her mother lived in Harold's Cross, Dublin.

1914: **Maggie Boyle**, 38 yrs, Prostitute from 57 Purdon Street. She was charged with larceny and sentenced to 6 weeks in prison.

1915: **Kate Blake**, 28 yrs, Prostitute from 3 Elliott Place.

1915: **Lizzie Byrne**, 27 yrs, Prostitute from 1 Elliott Place. Her sister is Mary Curley from 10 Linenhall Street.

C

1903: **Nanny Cleary**, 26 yrs, Prostitute from Purdon Street. She was born in New York,

1905: **Emily Carson**, 20 yrs, Prostitute from 8 Elliott Place. Charged with illegal possession of boots, 14 days. Born in Cork, her father is Michael Carson.

1905: **Bridget Crotty**, 30 yrs, Prostitute from 13 Elliott Place. She was born in Portlaw, County Waterford.

Enjoying a rest in the Monto

1905: **Kate Caulfield**, 24 yrs, Prostitute from 12 Elliott Place.

Charged with larceny in a brothel, discharged.

1906: **Annie Collins**, 21 yrs, Prostitute from 16 Elliott Place.

1913: **Maggie Clarke**, 24 yrs, Prostitute from 10 Elliott Place.
She was born in Bray, County Wicklow. Her father is John Clarke.

1915: **Jennie Creighton**, 35 yrs, Prostitute from 40 Purdon Street.
Habitually drunk.

1916: **Winifred Collins**, 18 yrs, Prostitute from 16 Elliott Place.

1917: **Cissy Carr**, 21 yrs, Prostitute from 12 Faithful Place.
Attempted suicide, 6 months, own bail of £5 pounds.

1917: **Annie Coffey/Lawlor**, 30 yrs, Prostitute from 51 Purdon
Street.
Born in Store Street, Dublin. Her father is Thomas Coffey from 14B
Corporation Buildings. She stole £31 pounds in a brothel, sentenced
to 6 months. There are two cut marks on her right arm.

1917: **Emily Carson**, 31 yrs, Prostitute from 15 Elliott Place.
She was born in Kingstown, County Dublin.

D

1901: **Anne Jane Doran/Weafer**, 34 yrs, Prostitute from 6 Purdon

Street. Her sister is Alice Kane from 33 Mabbott Street.

1905: **Esther Daly**, 21 yrs, Prostitute from 15 Elliott Place.

1905: **Annie Daly/Murphy**, 22 yrs, Prostitute from 15 Elliott Place.

Her sister lives on Summerhill.

1905: **Lizzie Dixon**, 22 yrs, Prostitute from 3 Elliott Place.

Born in Rathgar, Dublin, her mother is Mrs Brennan.

1905: **Delia Devlin**, 28 yrs, Prostitute from Purdon Street.

Delia was born in Belfast. She had brown hair and blue eyes.

1906: **Lilly Dixon**, 27 yrs, Prostitute from 14 Elliott Place.

1906: **Sarah Desmond**, 23 yrs, Prostitute from 13 Elliott Place. She was born in Cork.

The older a woman became the more unlikely it was that she could earn a good living on the street.

1911: **Minnie Doran**, 25 yrs, Prostitute from 12 Elliott Place.
She was up on a charge of larceny of a watch and chain.
Stole curtains, 6 months with hard labour.

1911: **Julia Doyle**, 42 yrs, Prostitute from 48 Purdon Street.

1913: **Ellen Donnolly**, 24 yrs, Prostitute from 40 Purdon Street.

1913: **Maggie Doolan**, 35 yrs, Prostitute from 3 Elliott Place.
She was born in Belfast.

1913: **Sarah Desmond alias Anne Clare alias Sarah Williams, alias Robinson alias Collins**, 40 yrs, Prostitute from 50 Elliott Place.
Tattoo on her left arm *"Matt Robinson"*.

1914: **Molly Doyle**, 23 yrs, Prostitute from 50 Purdon Street.

1915: **Essie Dorman**, 23 yrs, Prostitute from 13 Elliott Place.
She was charged with malicious damage, 2 months hard labour.

1915: **Violet Duinage**, 23 yrs, Prostitute from 5 Elliott Place.
She was sentenced to 14 days for soliciting. She was born in Galway.

1917: **Mary Donohe**, 30 yrs, Prostitute from 6 Elliott Place.

1917: **Minnie Doyle**, 30 yrs, Prostitute from 15 Elliott Place.

1918: **Connie Doherty**, Prostitute from 40 Purdon Street.

E

1906: **Maggie Early**, 26 yrs, Prostitute from 15 Elliott Place.
 Robbery with violence, 8 months in Mountjoy.

1911: **Cecelia Early**, 21 yrs, Prostitute from11 Elliott Place.

1916: **Mabel Ennis**, 32 yrs, Prostitute from 2 Elliott Place.

F

1903: **Molly Fanning,** 29 yrs, Prostitute from Faithful Place. She was born in England.

G

1905: **Lizzie Greekes/Russell**, Prostitute from 6 Faithful Place. She was born in County Cavan. Her sister, Nellie lived in 5 Elliott Place.

1905: **Jane Graham**, 22 yrs, Prostitute from 2 Elliott Place. She was born in Drogheda, County Louth. Her mother, Mary lves lives in Athlone, County Westmeath.

1907**:** **Jane Grehan**, 23 yrs, Prostitute from 16 Elliott Place.

1913: **Nellie Greekes**, 26 yrs, Prostitute from 5 Elliott Place. Mother is Margaret Farrelly from County Cavan.

H

1907: **Daisy Henderson**, 40 yrs, Prostitute from 40 Purdon Street. She was born in Dolphin's Barn, Dublin. She ran a Shebeen with her husband, James Spence in Gloucester Street.

1907: **Margaret Hutton/Scannell**, 34 yrs, Prostitute from Purdon Street. She was arrested for having sexual intercourse in a public place with James Murphy.

1910: **Lizzie Hickey**, 33 yrs, Prostitute from Elliott Place. She was born in Britain Street

1911: **Annie Holland**, 37 yrs, Prostitute from 10 Elliott Place. Larceny in a brothel.

1911: **Bridget Higgins**, 22 yrs, Prostitute from 15 Elliott Place.

1912: **Annie Houlahan/Maguire**, 24 yrs, Prostitute from 11 Elliott Place.

1914: **Lillie Holohan**, 20 yrs, Prostitute from 50 Purdon Street.

1914: **Harriet Hannon**, 19 yrs, Prostitute from 40 Purdon Street. Charged with attempted suicide, discharged.

1915: **Anne Harvey**, 40 yrs, Prostitute from 81 Purdon Street. Anne was born in Skerries, County Dublin.

1917: **Eliza Hamilton**, 40 yrs, from 11 Elliott Place. She was born in County Kildare.

A scene in Railway Street with clothes hanging on the railings to dry out in the morning sunshine.

J

1907: **Annie Johnston**, 23 yrs, Prostitute from 15 Elliott Place.
She was born in Nobber, County Meath. Her father is Bernard.

1907: **Kate Johnston**, 30 yrs, Prostitute from 14 Elliott Place.
She was born in Baldoyle, County Dublin.

1911: **Anne Fearn/Johnston**, 25 yrs, Prostitute from 40 Purdon Street.
Her father is Bernard Flanagan from Nobber, County Meath.

1914: **Jane Jones**, 33 yrs, Prostitute from 3 Elliott Place.

1915: **Emily Jackson**, 33 yrs, Prostitute from 3 Elliott Place.
Her mother is Mary Kenny from Tullow. Tattooed on her left arm are the words "Tom Pender".

1918: **Jennie Jones**, 39 yrs, Prostitute from 12 Elliott Place.

1918: **Agnes Jones**, 27 yrs, Prostitute from 3 Elliott Place.

1918: **Annie Joyce/Dempsey**, 26 yrs, Prostitute from 1 Elliott Place.
She was born in England. Her mother is Mary Joyce from Birr, County Offaly.

K

1906: **Margaret Kennedy**, 24 yrs, Prostitute from 2 Faithful Place.
She was born in County Wicklow, her mother is M.P. Kennedy. She was fined ten shillings for soliciting.

1906: **Nellie Kavanagh**, 27 yrs, Prostitute from 13 Elliott Place.
Larceny of a wristwatch.

1906: **Jane Kavanagh**, 27 yrs, Prostitute from 16 Elliott Place

1907: **Alice Kelly**, 22 yrs, Prostitute from 4 Elliott Place.

This young girl was a 'Monto Baby' who, at three years of age was found wandering the streets in search of a home.

1911: **Maggie Kelly**, 24 yrs, Prostitute from 11 Elliott Place.

She was born in North King Street. Her mother is Mary Kelly from Francis Street, Dublin.

1912: **Mary Kenny/Corrigan**, 26 yrs, Prostitute from 16 Elliott Place.

Her mother is Mary Corrigan from Gloucester Place.

1915: **Maggie Kenny**, 24 yrs, Prostitute from 11 Elliott Place.

1915: **Connie Kane**, 30 yrs, Prostitute from 15 Elliott Place.

1915: **Elizabeth Keating**, 26 yrs, Prostitute from 6 Elliott Place.

She stole a purse, 14 days.

1915: **Christina Kelly**, 21 yrs, Prostitute from 10 Elliott Place.

1916: **Emily Kavanagh**, 30 yrs, Prostitute from 3 Elliott Place.

1917: **Mary Kerins**, 38 yrs, Prostitute from 31 Purdon Street.

1918: **Mary Kelly**, 20 yrs, Prostitute from 1 Elliott Place.

She was born in Sheriff Street, Dublin. Her sister, Teresa Kelly lives in Rostrevor, County Down.

L

1903: **Lena Lewis**, 39 yrs, from Purdon Street.

She was born in Peter's Street, Dublin.

1905: **Kate Levingston**, 23 yrs, Prostitute from Faithful Place.

She has a tattoo on her left arm *"Harry and Rose"*. She was born in Rathkeale, County Limerick.

1906: **Agnes Lester**, 22 yrs, Prostitute from 50 Purdon Street.

She was born in Kingstown, County Dublin. Her brother is Jack Lester.

© Martin Coffey

*Unlike the younger girls, older prostitutes had little or no chance
of making a decent living on the streets.*

1906: **Kate Lyons**, 39 yrs, from Elliott Place.

1911: **Nellie Lynch**, 22 yrs, Prostitute from 12 Faithful Place.

1911: **Evelyn Lynch**, 22 yrs, Prostitute from 2 Faithful Place.
Charged with robbery.

1913: **Annie Lawlor/Coffey**, 28 yrs, Prostitute from 9 Elliott Place.

1915 **Annie Lynch**, 29 yrs, Prostitute from 11 Elliott Place.

M

1904, **Kate McDermot**, 33 yrs, Prostitute from Purdon Street.
She was born in Townsend Street, Dublin

1905: **Emily Mack/Macken**, 54 yrs, Prostitute from 15 Elliott Place.

1905: **Delia Murray**, 27 yrs, Prostitute from 51 Purdon Street.

1906: **Nellie Murphy**, Prostitute from 13 Elliott Place.

1907: **Mary G. Moore**, 32 yrs, Prostitute from 1 Faithful Place.

1907: **Nellie Morgan**, 28 yrs, Prostitute from 11 Elliott Place.
She was born in County Sligo

1907: **Lily Murphy**, 21 yrs, Prostitute from 14 Elliott Place.

1911: **Eva Murphy**, 27 yrs, Prostitute from 10 Elliott Place.
Larceny in a brothel.

1911: **Lily Morris**, 26 yrs, Prostitute from 3 Elliott Place

1911: **Margaret McCarthy**, 26 yrs, Prostitute from 3 Elliott Place.

1911: **Connie Murray**, 25 yrs, Prostitute from 8 Elliott Place.

1912: **Maggie McCarthy**, 26 yrs, Prostitute from 15 Elliott Place.
Larceny in a brothel.

1915: **Lilly Morris**, 26 yrs, Prostitute from 3 Elliott Place.

1915: **Nelly McNally**, 23 yrs, Prostitute from 10 Elliott Place.

Drink was very often the only company for the older prostitutes.

1915: **Rachel Martin**, 27 yrs, Prostitute from 1 Elliott Place.

Her father is John Martin from Tipperary.

1918: **Polly Moynete**, Prostitute from 12 Elliott Place.

N

1904: **Bridget Nutter nee Finn**, 28 yrs, Prostitute from Purdon Street.

1915: **Bridget Nolan**, 26 yrs, Prostitute from 11 Elliott Place.

Her mother is Mary Nolan from Templeogue, County Dublin.

O

1902: **Mary O'Brien,** 21 yrs, Prostitute, from Purdon Street.

She was born in Smithfield, Dublin.

1906: **Jennie O'Connor**, 22 yrs, Prostitute from 51 Purdon Street.

She was born in Meath Street and her sister is Essie King.

1908: **Anne O'Shea**, 29 yrs, Prostitute from 8 Elliott Place.

1915: **Molly O'Conner**, 24 yrs, Prostitute from 16 Elliott Place.

She was sentenced to 1 month for soliciting.

1907: **Anne O'Brien**, 29 yrs, Prostitute from 1 faithful Place.

R

1914: **Mary Ellen Reidy**, 38 yrs, Prostitute from 51 Purdon Street.

1915: **Hannah Rigney**, 26 yrs, Prostitute from 12 Elliott Place.

She was arrested for Illegal possession of butter, sentenced to one month in Mountjoy Gaol.

1915: **Kate Reilly**, 34 yrs, Prostitute from 21 Purdon Street.

Her sister, Mary Hand lives in Kilkenny.

1904: **Annie Sullivan/Gibney**, 32 yrs, Prostitute from Elliott Place.

A group of young boys from the Monto in 1929. One of the boys is barefooted and most of them are wearing caps.

S

1901: **Margaret Streeton**, 50 yrs, Prostitute from Faithful Place.
She was born in Cork and fined for selling unlicensed Porter.

1904: **Annie Brown/Gibney,** 32 years, Prostitute, Elliot Place.
She was born in Howth, County Dublin, where her brother lives.
She was fined ten shillings for soliciting.

1905: **Rebecca Smith**, 23 yrs, Prostitute from 13 Elliott Place.

1906: **Lizzie Sheehan**, 26 yrs, Prostitute from 15 Elliott Place.
Assault with larceny, 8 months.

1906: **Lily Smith**, 24 yrs, Prostitute from 7 Faithful Place.

1907: **Ellen Sterman**, 24 yrs, Prostitute from 13 Elliott Place.

1907: **Anne Sheridan**, 32 yrs, Prostitute from 1 Faithful Place. Larceny of watch, 6 months.

1911: **Mary Sheridan**, 20 yrs, Prostitute from 13 Elliott Place. Larceny of £11 pounds from a person.

1912: **Mary Staunton**, 25 yrs, Prostitute from 1 Elliott Place. Larceny in a brothel.

1912: **Mary Smith/Sweeney**, 37 yrs, Prostitute from 51 Purdon Street. She was born in Birr, County Offaly.

1914: **Lillie Snow**, 26 yrs, Prostitute from 1 Elliott Place.

1915: **Molly Smith**, 27 yrs, Prostitute from 11 Elliott Place. Born in Rush, County Dublin.

1917: **Cecelia Smith**, 30 yrs, Prostitute from 6 Elliott Place.

Purdon Street 1923.

Railway Street.

T

1905: **Lily Thompson**, 28 yrs, Prostitute from 40 Purdon Street.

1911: **Mary Tierney**. 17 yrs, Prostitute from 5 Elliott Place.

1911: **Annie Taylor**, 39 yrs, Prostitute from 2 Faithful Place.
Larceny in a brothel, 12 months.

1915: **Lily Traynor**, 37 yrs, Prostitute from 1 Elliott Place.
Her father is John Traynor. In 1921 Lily Traynor was arrested for being outdoors without a permit. She was fined 7 shillings and 6 pennies. She was still living in number 1 Elliott Place

1915: **Bridget Tyrrell**, 31 yrs, Prostitute from 15 Elliott Place.
She was sentenced to 1 month for soliciting. Her father is
Michael Tyrrell from Athy in County Kildare.

1912: **Anne Taylor**, 40 yrs, Prostitute from 16 Elliott Place.

An old Monto Madam and her dog.

U

1904: **Mabel Uzell,** 34 yrs, Prostitute from Purdon Street.

She was born in Dunshaughlin, County Meath.

V

1916: **Mary Vincent,** 29 yrs, Prostitute from 5 Elliott Place.

She was originally an abandoned baby. She lived with her adopted family in Templeogue, County Dublin.

W

1914: **Lillie Watson**, Prostitute from 51 Purdon Street.

1905: **Agnes Williams**, Prostitute from 2 Elliott Place.

1905: **Mabel Watson**, 30 yrs old, Prostitute from 16 Elliott Place.

1905: **Rose Wilson**, 22 yrs, Prostitute from 6 Elliott Place.

1906: **Mary White**, 36 yrs, Prostitute from 58 Purdon Street.

1907: **Maud Wood**, 25 yrs, Prostitute from 11 Elliott Place.

Born in County Longford. Her brother is Frank McGowan, living on the North Strand in Dublin.

1907: **Emily Woods**, 27 yrs, Prostitute from Elliott Place.

She was born in Kingstown, County Dublin. Her mother is Lizzie Woods from England.

1907: **Kathleen Williams**, 29 yrs, Prostitute from 2 Faithful Place.

She was born on the South Circular Road, Dublin, fined ten shillings for soliciting.

1911: **Kate Ward/Warner**, 24 yrs, Prostitute from 3 Elliott Place.

She was born in Mullingar, County Westmeath. Her father is William Warner.

1911: **Sarah Williams**, 40 yrs, Prostitute from 12 Faithful Place.

1917: **Olive Yeates**, 20 yrs, Prostitute from 1 Faithful Place.

A Dublin tenement doorway.

Reference

All prison related materials and photographs as indicated in this publication in relation to Mountjoy Prison, Maryboro Prison, Kilmainham Jail and Grangegorman Female Penitentiary are copyrighted exclusively to the National Archives and are published with the permission of the Director of the National Archives, Ireland.

The following are the names and reference numbers of the prison records, as found in the National Archives Ireland collection.

Nannie McLoughlin GPB/PEN/1901/42

Margaret Carroll GPB/PEN/1901/76

John Byrne GPB/PEN/1903/95

Anne Higgins GPB/PEN/3/ 152

John McLoughlin GPB/PEN/3/157

Other publications by this author

Growing up in a family of 15 children

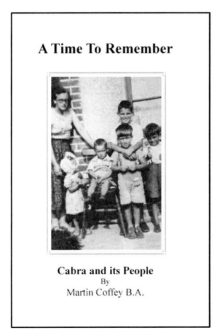

A social history of Cabra and its People

A collection of stories and photographs of Cabra West

A life-time of Neil Diamond

A Dubliner's photographic collection

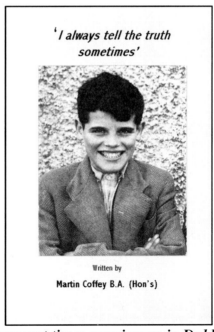

Innocent times growing up in Dublin

The author was also involved in the following publications.

Belvedere Newsboys' Club 2009

A very positive success story 2016
Paddy McEvoy